W9-ANX-590

CONTENTS

1. **Introducing Vietnam** 5
   The Land 6
   History in Brief 11
   Government and Economy 22
   The People 25

2. **Hanoi** 35
   Orientation 36
   Hoan Kiem District and
   Old Hanoi 36
   Ba Dinh District and the
   West Lake 40
   Southeast of Hoan
   Kiem Lake 43
   Day Excursions from Hanoi 44

3. **The North** 49
   East of Hanoi 50
   North of Hanoi 53
   South of Hanoi 55

4. **Central Vietnam:**
   Hue to Da Nang 61
   Hue 62
   Hue's Citadel 65
   South of Hue's River 70
   Hue's Imperial Tombs 71
   Da Nang 74
   Around Da Nang 77

5. **Nha Trang and the**
   Central Highlands 85
   Nha Trang 86
   Nha Trang Sights 87
   Excursions from
   Nha Trang 89
   Da Lat 91
   Da Lat Sights 92
   Around Da Lat 94

6. **Ho Chi Minh City**
   (Saigon) 97
   City Sights 98
   Ho Chi Minh City
   Pagodas 101
   Cholon 103
   Day Excursions from
   Ho Chi Minh City 105

7. **The Mekong Delta** 111
   Exploring the
   Mekong Delta 111
   My Tho 115
   Vinh Long 116
   Can Tho 116
   Long Xuyen 117
   Chau Doc 118
   Rach Gia 119
   Ha Tien 120

Travel Tips 122

Index 127

1
Introducing Vietnam

Vietnam is strikingly beautiful – a country whose very existence is dominated by water; monsoons, floods, rivers and seas.

Up and down the land, rice paddies – at varying stages of growth – create a kaleidoscope of greens. Watery ribbons of newly planted paddies reflect the mountains and women in conical hats complete the animated oriental Lowry tableau.

In the north, sailing junks have disappeared from **Ha Long Bay** – motors are so much easier for the fishermen and their families who live on board, but picturesque, slim slivers of boats driven by a single, foot-powered paddle, still skim the rivers and bays.

Splendid red- and gold-lacquered pavilions and pleasure gardens line the banks of the **Perfume River** in **Hue** as relics of the last imperial capital. Further south at **Nha Trang**, fishermen paddle out to boats in tiny, tarred basket-boats and fish with huge shimmering nets that turn to gold in the evening sun. In the **Mekong Delta**, dense palms crowd the banks of the narrow canals and little boys leap off flimsy bamboo bridges.

The streets in the cities, that were once a swarm of bicycles, now throb with the roar of motorbikes. Glass and steel towers, new joint-venture hotels and mini-hotels have shot up amongst the old shophouses selling electrical and electronic goods. Internet cafés have replaced photo labs and photocopy shops as trendy new businesses, and charming new restaurants and smart new **resorts** have also opened.

Opposite: *Thien Mu (Pagoda of the Heavenly Lady) built in 1660, in Hue.*

WHEN TO VISIT VIETNAM

Given the considerable regional climatic variation, there is no single best time to visit Vietnam. The later months are generally best in the south, particularly the coolish, dry months of December and January. The **north** is most pleasant in September and October, and March and April. Heavy rains fall in **Hanoi** in July and August, in **Hue** in September and October and in the **south** from June to August.

Today the country is rushing headlong towards **consumerism** – racing to catch up with other lands. The poor, hardy Vietnamese who have struggled and endured so much for so long are at last seeing their lives improve little by little.

Vietnam's young – more than two-thirds of the population are under 30 – clamour for Western fashions, football, disco music and karaoke. But amidst these changes, the people tenaciously hold to their **traditional** values: the strength and responsibility of family ties, respect for elders, a reverence for education and scholarship and a deep-rooted politeness.

Pizza may have arrived, but Vietnam's delicious universal noodle soup (*pho*) is still served in steaming bowls in pavement cafés. Along the coast, giant shrimps are still grilled in sea salt and garlic and at **Nha Trang**, seafood and rice are still cooked in coconut shells.

For the visitor, Vietnam offers numerous unique experiences. Only in Vietnam can one see **water puppets** (colourful carved floating dolls) dexterously manipulated by underwater bamboo poles, or hear the soulful wail of the one-stringed *dan bau* instrument, the hollow whisper of the giant bamboo xylophone, the *lem trung*, and the howl of Hue singing, while floating on a boat down the **Perfume River**. Only in Vietnam can one chortle at the tragi-farcical musical theatre, *cai leung*. The Vietnamese are a nation of poets and singers, passionate in their love of bright colours and costumes. Surprisingly, considering their grievous experience of successive **wars**, the Vietnamese are openly friendly to foreigners and a disarmingly warm and emotional people, eager to welcome visitors to their country of which they are so proud.

THE LAND

Vietnam is a long thin country stretching 3260km (2037 miles) along the eastern coast of the Indo-Chinese peninsula on the South China Sea. The Vietnamese visualize their country as a long thin carrying pole with two rice baskets: in the north the **Red River Valley**, in the south the **Mekong Delta**. At its narrowest it measures only 50km (30 miles) wide. It covers an area of 330,363km² (127,520 square miles), roughly the size of Italy.

Vietnam divides into three distinct areas: the **highlands** and Red River Delta of the north; the **Truong Son Mountains** and coastal plains linking north to south; and the Mekong Delta in the south. These divisions are known as **Bac Bo**, **Trung Bo** and **Nam Bo**, which correspond to the former French colonial districts of Tonkin, Annam and Cochinchina.

In the north, running from northwest to southeast, is the area's most important valley. Known as **Song Hong** in Vietnamese, the Red River rises in China's Yunnan province and flows through northern Vietnam, where the delta, a flat triangular region of some 3000km² (1158 square miles), which was once an inlet of the Gulf of Tonkin, has filled up over the millennia with alluvial deposits. A lush and fertile region, it is the ancestral home of the ethnic Vietnamese and location of the nation's capital, **Hanoi**.

In its central region, Vietnam forms a long thin crescent, fringed by a narrow coastal plain and backed by the Truong Son Mountains running from north to south. These mountains, which have several plateaux, are broken by west-east spurs that divide the coastal strip into valleys. In the southern part of the area are the **Central Highlands** (Tay Nguyen), some 51,800km² (20,000 square miles) of rugged mountain peaks, extensive forests and fertile red soil.

ROUND VIETNAM

A full north to south tour of the country is recommended for the first-time visitor. With a minimum of 15 days, an itinerary might include: Hanoi, the historic and present capital; Hue, the last imperial capital; Hoi An (near Da Nang), the ancient port of the Chams; Nha Trang, for its fine beaches; Mui Ne, a new beach resort; Ho Chi Minh City (Saigon) and the Mekong Delta. With a minimum of 10 days, and concentrating on the north, an itinerary might include Hanoi, Hue, Da Nang and Hoi An; a trip to the south may include Ho Chi Minh City, the Mekong Delta, Mui Ne, Da Lat and Nha Trang. Transport could be a combination of plane, car, bus and train. It is best to fly from Hanoi to Hue, and from Da Nang to Nha Trang, making the rest of the journey by hired car (with a driver), by tour bus or train. Main roads, such as Highway 1, which links Hanoi to Ho Chi Minh City, are continually being improved, but still remain below Western motorway standards.

Left: The Mekong Delta is justifiably known as the nation's 'rice bowl', producing over half the country's annual needs.

Right: *Everyone's image of a tropical beach – Vietnam is perhaps less well known for its several coastal resorts.*

The southeastern shoulder of the country is surprisingly arid, in certain places giving rise to sand dunes that might have been lifted from the Sahara. Dominating the southwest is the **Mekong Delta**, which covers an area of about 40,000km^2 (15,440 square miles) and comprises a vast, flat alluvial plain where no point is more than 3m (9ft) above sea level. The Mekong is the world's 12th-longest river, running 4200km (2625 miles) from the Tibetan mountains through China, Myanmar (once Burma), Laos, Thailand and Cambodia to South China Sea at Vietnam's southernmost tip. At the northeastern apex of this intensely fertile delta is **Ho Chi Minh City** (previously known as Saigon), the country's largest metropolis.

A number of **offshore islands** in the Gulf of Thailand and in the South China Sea form part of Vietnam's territorial claims, including the **Paracel Islands** and the **Spratly Islands**, for which sovereignty is disputed by several neighbouring countries.

Climate

Vietnam has a **tropical monsoon climate** with high humidity year-round. The two monsoon seasons – the northeast monsoon blows from November to April and the southwest monsoon blows from May to October – are rendered almost totally meaningless by regional differences governed by **altitude**, **mountain passes** that block the weather and the distance from north to south. Suffice it to say that annual **rainfall** is substantial (so bring along an umbrella), ranging from 120cm (47in) to 300cm (118in), with 90 per cent of the rain falling between May and November in most places.

In Hanoi temperatures average 16°C (61°F) in winter and 30°C (86°F) in summer. The hottest months are from April to September, the coldest are from December to March and the rainiest are July and August.

In the south, the seasonal differences are defined more as dry and wet than cold and hot. Annual temperatures average 27–31°C (80–88°F), the hottest months being from March to May, the coolest being December and January and the rainiest from April to October.

In central Vietnam, coastal regions are subject to typhoons in the summer, the hottest months are from April to September, the coolest from December to April and the rainiest from September to November. The central highlands are noted for a cool, almost temperate climate right through the year.

Flora and Fauna

Originally, the entire Indo-Chinese peninsula was **tropical** rainforest. In 1943, Vietnam's forests totalled

DISAPPEARING FORESTS

A significant contribution to forest depletion is made by the practice of shifting, slash-and-burn cultivation in the highlands of Vietnam. As a consequence, the soil becomes degraded, which inhibits the forests' ability to grow back. Logging also poses a serious threat, and the export of logs and timber has been banned in an effort to reduce further forest loss.

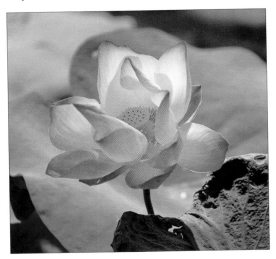

Left: *Despite ecological devastation during the Vietnam War, over 700 plant species continue to add colour, including the delicate lotus flower.*

13 million ha (32 million acres) – 42 per cent of national
territory. By 1982 the forests had shrunk to 7.8 million
ha (19 million acres), about 23 per cent of the land
area, due to colonial policies, wars, slash-and-burn
agriculture and rapid population growth. Through the
efforts of the government's **reforestation** programme, it
was estimated by 1999 that forests extended over
approximately 28 per cent of the land, but of this, only
10 per cent remains as primary **rainforest**.

There have been other gains – the U-Minh forest in
the Mekong Delta has largely been rescued from the
ravages of chemical defoliants and it is now the world's
largest **mangrove swamp** outside the Amazon basin.

The National Conservation Strategy calls for the
creation of more than 100 **protected areas** in addition
to the already existing 11 **national parks**. The most accessible of these are **Cat Ba National Park**, occupying half a

large island 30km (18 miles) off the coast of Haiphong; **Ba Be**, north of Hanoi; **Cuc Phuong**, southeast of Hanoi; **Bach Ma**, near Hue in central Vietnam and in the southern central highlands, **Nam Cat Tien** and **Yok Don**.

Vietnam's flora and fauna are also diminishing. The country boasts some 12,000 species of plants, many of which have commercial value such as hardwoods, medicinal plants and sources of resins. Fauna, which numbers 273 species of **mammals**, 180 species of **reptiles** and over 800 species of **birds**, is sadly declining as natural habitats are being destroyed. Among the larger animals endangered are elephants, rhinos, tigers, mountain leopards, black bears, deer and certain species of monkeys.

HISTORY IN BRIEF

More than perhaps any other people, the Vietnamese have forged their national identity through centuries of almost constant struggle against one opposing force or another. The principal **battles** have been against domination by China (Vietnam's huge northern neighbour from whom it derives much of its cultural influence), and against natural barriers in a gradual expansion southwards from an original heartland in the Red River Delta, across the mountain spurs of the central part of the country and into the extensive flatlands of the Mekong Delta. The fact that the Vietnamese have maintained a distinct cultural heritage speaks volumes for their strength of national character.

The precise origins of the Vietnamese are lost in the mists of **mythology**. It is known that the earliest human habitation in the fertile plains of the Red River Delta probably dates back to Palaeolithic times. The first discernible lineage with today's peoples, however, did not begin to emerge until the late Neolithic period, early Bronze Age, when the Phung Nguyen culture was centred in modern-day Vinh Phu Province, northwest of Hanoi, from ca. 2000 to 1400BC. The development of wet-rice cultivation and bronze casting in the Red and Ma river plains from about 1200BC, gave rise to the

Opposite: *Over 17,000km (10,600 miles) of Vietnam's inland waterways are navigable, although not always all year round. The Mekong Delta is less prone to flooding than its Red River counterpart in the north.*

LEGENDARY PAST

The Dong Son culture is linked in Vietnamese traditions with the semi-legendary Hung dynasty (mythological dates 2879–258BC) and the kingdom of Van Lang. The founder of the dynasty is held to be Hung Vuong, the son of Lac Long Quan – the Lac dragon king who taught the people the technique of wet-rice cultivation. Irrigated rice fields were called lac fields and, according to Chinese annals, the people were identified as Lac Viets, whom the Vietnamese recognize as their direct ancestors.

Below Right: *China's impact on Vietnamese culture and religion is evident in Hanoi's Temple of Literature, dedicated to Confucius.*

sophisticated Dong Son culture, best known for its elaborate bronze drums (on display in the History Museums, Hanoi and Ho Chi Minh City).

Chinese Rule

It is believed that the Lac Viets occupied the northern delta plains and that a kingdom called **Au Lac** existed, although its boundaries are unknown. Some kind of **feudal** union probably prevailed until local power was gradually eroded by incursions from **Nam Viet**, a kingdom founded in 208BC by the Chinese general Trieu Da, that extended over much of what is now southern China. The Lac lords continued to rule in the Red River Delta but as vassals of Nam Viet, which held sway over the area for a century, while remaining on uneasy and constantly shifting terms with China.

1000 YEARS OF CHINESE RULE

During Chinese domination revolt only served to make life more difficult – forced labour, the burning of Vietnamese libraries, and ceaseless, burdensome demands for tribute were typical. An ironic reflection on the state of affairs is found in the name the Chinese gave Vietnam in the late 7th century – *Annam*, meaning the 'Pacified South'.

HISTORICAL CALENDAR

ca. 2000–1400BC Early Bronze Age Phung Nguyen culture.

1200BC Development of wet-rice cultivation and bronze casting.

208BC Foundation of the Kingdom of Nam Viet.

111BC Chinese gain control of Red River Delta from Nam Viet.

AD39 Trung sisters lead ultimately unsuccessful revolt against Chinese rule.

939 After defeat of Chinese, Ngo Quyen founds first national dynasty.

1009 Founding of Le dynasty; southward expansion begins.

1010 Capital moved to Hanoi.

1070 Founding of first university, the Temple of Literature in Hanoi.

1225 Tran dynasty succeeds Le dynasty.

1257, 1284, 1287 Mongol invaders successfully resisted.

1407–28 Renewal of Chinese domination after collapse of Ho dynasty.

1428 Late Le dynasty founded after Le Loi overthrows Chinese rulers.

1471 Conquest of Champa Kingdom finally completed.

1771–1802 Tay Son peasant rebellion marks end of Late Le dynasty and unification of Vietnam.

1802 Prince Nguyen Anh as Gia Long proclaims himself emperor of the Kingdom of Vietnam and is installed in Hue.

1862 Cochinchina created as a French colony.

1883 Central and northern Vietnam set up as French protectorates, named Annam and Tonkin.

1890 Birth of Ho Chi Minh.

1924 Association of Revolutionary Youth, later the Indo-Chinese Communist Party, founded by Ho Chi Minh to oppose colonial rule.

1945 Ho Chi Minh declares himself president of an independent Vietnam on 2 September. French refuse to give up colonial possessions, leading to First Indo-China War (1945–1954).

1954 French defeat at Dien Bien Phu ends colonial rule. Geneva agreement provisionally divides country at 17th parallel. Ngo Dinh Diem takes power in South, ending hopes for peaceful reunification.

1960 Formation of National Front for the Liberation of South Vietnam (NLF) prompts increased US involvement and the start of the Second Indo-China War (1965-75)

1969 Ho Chi Minh dies.

1975 War ends with North victorious over South. Reunification follows.

1986 Official government policy of *doi moi* (new thinking) introduced.

1994 US lifts Vietnamese trade embargo.

1995 Full diplomatic relations established between Hanoi and Washington.

2002 Trade agreement ratified between Vietnam and US.

At the same time, China was becoming reorganized under the **Han dynasty** (206BC–AD220). In 111BC, the army of Han Emperor Wu Di defeated Nam Viet and succeeded in gaining control over the Red River Delta. There followed nearly 1000 years of **Chinese rule**, when the Lac Viets were governed, with varying degrees of severity and resistance, as a province of China.

Although China's domination was prolonged and its cultural influence indelible, the Vietnamese never willingly accepted the situation. Several rebellions and uprisings during the millennium of Chinese rule took place, setting a historical pattern of mutual **antagonism**

MISNOMER

The word 'Funan' is the Chinese mispronunciation of the word *bnam* (*phnom* in modern Khmer), meaning 'mountain'. It was not the name of the country, which is unknown, but rather the title taken by its rulers, *kurung bnam*, 'King of the Mountain'.

that has never entirely vanished. Forcible attempts to Sinicize the local culture were resisted, but the Lac Viets inevitably underwent permanent change while under the Chinese yoke. Exposure to **Confucianism** was particularly influential, and the later evolution of Vietnamese administration, law, education, literature, language and culture generally displays pronounced Chinese elements. The indigenous **culture** of the ordinary people was to a great extent preserved, but the ruling elite were profoundly affected and later maintained a deep admiration for Chinese culture which, nonetheless, always stopped short of willing acceptance of Chinese political control.

It is from such an involved history of socio-political evolution that Vietnam gradually developed its complex national character, partly moulded by Chinese cultural influences – Buddhist, Taoist, Confucianist – and partly by a powerful nationalist and militaristic force generated by the struggle for national survival.

Funan and Champa

Chinese sovereignty never extended beyond what is now northern Vietnam, and the southern and central parts of the country were subject, respectively, to a separate historical development under distinct civilizations.

Opposite: *Temple remains in the ancient Cham principality of Phan Rang, central Vietnam.*
Right: *Java-influenced stone carving on display at Da Nang's Museum of Cham Sculpture.*

In the south, the earliest non-Vietnamese civilization was the kingdom of Funan, centred on the Mekong Delta. Probably inhabited mostly by people of the **Mon-Khmer** group, Funan is thought to have been founded sometime during the 1st century AD, though evidence is scant and the only historical accounts are Chinese chronicles, the earliest of which mentions **Funan** in the 2nd century.

The records of a 3rd-century Chinese embassy give a physical sense of place: 'There are walled villages, palaces and dwellings. The men are ugly and black, and their hair is frizzy; they go about naked and barefoot. They are simple by nature. Taxes are paid in gold, silver and perfume. There are books and libraries and they use an alphabet.'

To the Chinese all foreigners were **barbarians** and this prejudice doubtlessly explains the unflattering description. But the Chinese mention of taxes, libraries and an alphabet implies cultural influences from India – historians recognize a pattern of 'Indianization' affecting most of Southeast Asia at this time. Such influence was intensified later when rulers came directly from India. One 5th-century Chinese source tells of bronze images of Indian gods, and describes the king as sitting in a classical Indian posture.

The extent of Funan's power is unclear; 20th-century excavations at Oc-Eo (thought to be the kingdom's major port, located near the Mekong Delta's west coast) suggest a seafaring people engaged in extensive **trade**. Aerial photographs taken in the 1930s revealed the sites of hundreds of Funanese settlements, along with traces of ancient **irrigation** canals.

Funan eventually lost its pre-eminence and its territory was taken over by the pre-Angkor Khmer kingdom of Chenla, and subsequently by Angkor itself. The Khmer were later to be ousted by the Vietnamese, although Khmer Krom (southern Khmer) still inhabit parts of the Mekong Delta.

Central Vietnam also has its own distinctive early **history** as the realm of the once powerful Hindu

CHAMPA KINGDOM

Occupying coastal territory north of the Mekong Delta, and with capitals at Hue, Da Nang, Binh Dinh and Phan Rang, the Indianized Champa civilization first emerged in the 2nd century AD. It comprised four states: from north to south, Amaravati (Quang Nnam-Da Nang), Vijaya (Binh Dinh), Kauthara (Nha Trang) and Panduranga (Phan Rang). Each, in that order, ultimately fell to the Vietnamese in the course of 14 centuries. A largely maritime people, the Cham were culturally and linguistically close to the Javanese. The civilization, which peaked in the 10th and 11th centuries, has all but vanished today, remembered in a scattering of tiered brick towers and some exquisite stone carvings.

Kingdom of Champa. Like Funan, Champa was an 'Indianized' maritime state, first rising to prominence in the late 2nd century AD in the region around what is now the town of Da Nang. It remained a powerful force in the region until it was conquered by the Vietnamese in the 15th century.

Above: *Founded in 1070, Hanoi's Temple of Literature is said to have been fashioned after a temple in Shantung, birthplace of Confucius.*

Independence from China

The end of foreign rule over northern Vietnam was signalled by the collapse of China's **Tang dynasty** at the end of the 10th century AD. So weakened, the Chinese occupiers were defeated in the battle of **Bach Dang River** in 938, after which the Vietnamese General Ngo Quyen founded the first national dynasty. There followed a brief period of **anarchy** and then subsequent weak,and usually shortlived, reigns. It was not until 1009 that a firm government was established with the founding of the **Le dynasty**.

The first 100 years of the new Le dynasty witnessed warfare not only with China in the north, but with the Khmer and the Chams to the south. Despite the conflicts, in 1070 the country's first university, the **Temple of Literature** in Hanoi, was founded. Once external threats had been dealt with, the second century of Le rule was a period of relative **peace**, during which the nation made considerable gains – administration was reorganized, public works undertaken, and agriculture was developed.

The Le dynasty also witnessed the beginning of Vietnam's southward **expansion**, prompted by population pressure. In 1079, the Cham were forced to cede their three northern provinces and Vietnamese peasants began occupying formerly untilled lands, turning them into rice fields. Thus a pattern was set for the long march south that would eventually lead to the Mekong Delta and, in the process, the final defeat of the Cham and the Khmer.

THE TRUNG SISTERS

In AD39 Trung Trac (the wife of a Lac king who had been executed by the Chinese) and her sister Trung Nhi led a revolt that held out against the Chinese for two years. When they were finally defeated the Trung sisters refused to surrender and committed suicide by drowning. Celebrated as Vietnamese heroines, they exemplify the relatively high status of women in Vietnam.

In 1225, a lord of the **Tran** family replaced the Le through marriage and founded a new dynasty (1225–1400) under which the country was further developed by improved **administration** and **land reforms**. The Tran were also notable for their military campaigns against the Mongols and the Cham. Invasions by the Mongol armies of Kublai Khan were successfully repulsed in 1257, 1284 and 1287. In the 14th century the Tran became engaged in wars against the Cham and although they experienced both successes and reversals, the march south continued.

By the beginning of the 15th century the Tran dynasty had declined and was overthrown by the shortlived **Ho dynasty** (1400–7). In 1407, internal turmoil opened the door for renewed Chinese domination and the **Ming dynasty** ruled Vietnam harshly as if it were a province of China for the next 20 years.

In 1428 **Le Loi**, one of Vietnam's most celebrated heroes, liberated the country from Chinese domination and founded the Late **Le dynasty**. The country now experienced a golden age, particularly under the greatest of the dynasty's rulers, **Le Thanh Tong** (1460–97), during whose reign important administrative and land reforms were effected. The conquest of the Kingdom of Champa was also finally accomplished in 1471.

The Le dynasty degenerated in the 15th century and although it lingered until it was ultimately overthrown by the **Tay Son rebellion** in the 1770s, unified rule throughout the country was at best tenuous, as the power of the dynastic **monarchs** was diminished by rival clans competing for supremacy. From the 16th century onwards, two of these clans – the **Trinh** in the north and the **Nguyen** in the south – divided control of the country

VIETNAMESE DYNASTIES
Ngo dynasty: 939–968
Dinh dynasty: 968–980
Early Le dynasty: 980–1009
Le dynasty: 1009–1225
Tran dynasty: 1225–1400
Ho dynasty: 1400–1407
Chinese rule: 1407–1428
Late Le dynasty: 1428–1776 (nominal after 1527)
Tay Son rebellion: 1771–1802
Nguyen dynasty: 1802–1945 (nominal after 1883)

Below: *A colourful mural in Hanoi depicts a Tran victory over 13th-century Mongol invaders.*

Below: *Pilgrims flock to Ho Chi Minh's Masoleum, based on the design for Lenin's tomb in Moscow.*

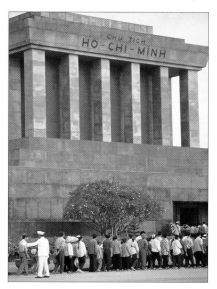

between them. During this time, with the Chams no longer a military force, the Nguyen continued Vietnam's southward drive, extending their influence into the Mekong Delta, where they wrested control from the Khmer and succeeded in establishing the southernmost limits of the nation by the late 18th century.

Arrival of the Europeans

Portuguese traders were the first Westerners on the scene, arriving in the early 16th century, followed by the **Dutch**. Trade contacts were shortlived, so European interests were left largely in the hands of **missionaries**, whose impact added a further dimension to the complexity of power struggles.

Predominantly **French** by the 18th century, the missionaries increasingly persuaded the French government to take a more political and military role in Vietnam in view of the unstable situation. The **Tay Son rebellion** (1771–1802) marked the final demise of the Le dynasty, as well as the overthrow of the Trinh and, temporarily, the Nguyen.

The rebellion, although initially successful, plunged the war-ravaged country into disarray, with factionalism persisting until the end of the 18th century. It was then that the one surviving Nguyen Lord, **Prince Nguyen Anh**, played into the hands of the future colonial power by seeking military aid from a French mission. He succeeded in raising an **army** against the Tay Son rebels, defeating them finally in 1801. A year later, Nguyen Anh changed his name to Gia Long, pronounced himself emperor of the Kingdom of Vietnam (the first use of the country's modern name), and installed himself in the Imperial City of **Hue**.

Under the **Nguyen dynasty** (1802–1945) founded by Gia Long, Vietnam was unified and ruled strictly according to the conservative, Chinese-influenced Confucian model. The absolute power of the government, however, was soon to be eroded by **French colonial interests**. Gia Long had rewarded French traders for their assistance during the Tay Son rebellion, but his successors reversed the policy and also took a repressive stance towards the European missionaries. This simply served to fuel France's growing involvement in the country.

Above: *A colonial-era government building in Hanoi presents a contrast in architectural style.*

Colonial Rule

In a series of military expeditions, beginning in 1847 at Da Nang, the French set about carving out a **colonial empire** in Indo-China. First southern Vietnam, Cochinchina, was formally created as a colony under direct administration in 1862 and subsequently, in 1883, the centre and northern parts of the country were set up as protectorates and respectively named Annam and Tonkin. A few years later the French consolidated effective control of the entire region with the creation of the **Indo-Chinese Union** comprising Cambodia and Laos as well as the three divisions of Vietnam.

Colonial rule brought some benefits – mainly in agricultural and infrastructure development – but mostly it sowed the seeds of discontent that would eventually yield a bitter harvest. Higher taxes and repressive rural landlords, in particular, served to disrupt the traditional equilibrium of village life. Thus the ground was prepared for **communism** to appear as the only effective challenge to the French. Founded

NAME CHANGE

The name Vietnam translates as 'the *Viet* people of the south (*nam*)', and it was adopted in the early 19th century by Emperor Gia Long. He had initially decided on 'Nam Viet' but the emperor of China, whose approval was sought, feared it might be confused with a similarly named ancient kingdom, which had included parts of China, so he reversed the words to Viet Nam.

Above: *Former enemies can come face to face in a process of reconciliation.*

and led by **Ho Chi Minh**, Vietnamese communism preached a patriotic anti-colonialism policy and called for a peasant revolution.

Communist opposition faced severe repression during the 1930s, until **World War II** radically altered the balance of power. Through an agreement between France's Vichy government and the Japanese, a façade of French colonial rule was maintained throughout most of the war. But, in March 1945, the Japanese deposed the French and installed **Emperor Bao Dai** as head of a nominally independent Vietnam. Bao Dai later abdicated in favour of **Ho Chi Minh** who, in the early 1940s, had established the League for the Independence of Vietnam, Viet Minh for short.

In spite of opposition from the Viet Minh, France refused to give up the colonial possessions it had; in its opinion they were only temporarily lost during World War II. This led to a protracted war – the **First Indo-China War** – which became another arena for the **Cold War**, with China and the **USSR** backing the Viet Minh and the **USA** giving financial support to France. On the battlefield France suffered a humiliating defeat at Dien Bien Phu in 1954, but peace talks in Geneva ended inconclusively with the two sides agreeing to regroup either side of a provisional ceasefire line drawn along the 17th parallel. The French and the USA, however, refused to sign political accords that would have provided for general elections. Vietnam had achieved **independence** but effectively was divided into two countries, North and South Vietnam. When the intransigent Ngo Dinh Diem took power in the South, replacing Bao Dai, any hope of a peaceful reunification was dashed.

Diem's administration was particularly **repressive** against members of the Viet Minh who had stayed in the South, while his narrowly-based policies in general alienated certain sections of the southern population,

Ho Chi Minh

Ho Chi Minh was born Nguyen Tat Thanh to a mandarin family in 1890 in the northern province of Nghe Tinh. After 13 years abroad he returned to Vietnam in 1924 and founded the Association of Revolutionary Youth, to become the Indo-Chinese Communist Party in 1930. Later spells were spent in Moscow and China. On 2 September 1945 he declared himself president of an independent Vietnam, so beginning the nationalist struggles against France and later US-backed South Vietnam. Ho Chi Minh died in 1969.

notably the peasantry and the Buddhists. The North (itself according harsh treatment to its dissenters) developed a strategy for involvement in the south and, in 1960, the National Front for the Liberation of South Vietnam (NLF) was formed to oppose Diem. This in turn prompted escalating US involvement in South Vietnam during the 1960s, first through so-called aid and finally through the commitment of combat troops. So began the **Second Indo-China War** – a well-documented episode of modern history. The dead (or missing in action) totalled 58,000 American personnel, 224,000 South Vietnamese soldiers, 1 million North Vietnamese and VC soldiers and nearly 4 million civilians – about 10 per cent of the population.

The tragedy ended in 1975 with the North's victory over the South and the subsequent reunification of Vietnam. The predicted bloodbath did not follow, although tens of thousands of officials, soldiers and other likely opposition were sent to 're-education' camps, some for 10 years and more. Huge numbers of **refugees** fled, some making desperate bids for freedom by fleeing Vietnam in small boats and many falling prey to pirates in the South China Sea. In an effort to halt the tragedy of the 'boat people', the USA set up an **Orderly Departure Programme** (ODP) which made provision for eligible political refugees (as opposed to economic refugees) to resettle in the West.

SYMBOLIC BRIDGE

Long Bien (Doumer) Bridge, the oldest of Hanoi's two spans across the Red River, became a symbol of resistance during the Vietnam War. Completed in 1902, the strategic 1682m (5519ft) bridge suffered nearly 200 sorties by US bombers but after every attack the Vietnamese managed to make repairs and keep the bridge open.

Below: *Lottery ticket vendors in Hanoi's old quarter. Vietnam's policy of renovation brings fresh economic challenges.*

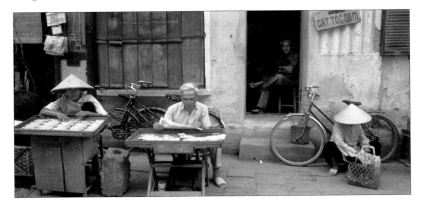

FACING THE FUTURE

As part of its policy of reconstruction, Vietnam has moved away from a planned economy towards a more market-based economic system. The introduction of laws granting legal recognition to private business has expanded economic activity in the private sector, while agriculture has been decollectivized.

Opposite: *Roll your own – tobacco is stacked and ready for sale in Lam Dong Province, southern Vietnam.*
Below: *Sea products are an important source of foreign exchange. Leading exports are crude oil and rice, along with textiles and processed foods.*

The Vietnamese government's attempts to rebuild the country after decades of war were slow. The first 10 years of peace under hard-line communist rule were largely a failure, and gains on social, political and economic fronts have been discernible only since 1986 when the government adopted a policy of renovation (*doi moi*). In the early 1990s the pace of change and **progress** began to accelerate at an unprecedented rate – limited only by a burdensome bureaucracy that has yet to be streamlined.

GOVERNMENT AND ECONOMY

Following the Vietnam War, the Democratic Republic of (North) Vietnam and the Republic of (South) Vietnam were formally **united** on 2 July 1976, to form the present nation of the **Socialist Republic of Vietnam**. In broad colouring, politics are Marxist-Leninist and rule is dominated by the Vietnamese Communist Party. In practice, government has been variously tailored to suit local needs and it has evolved to a certain extent in recent years.

Vietnam has had four constitutions, respectively adopted in 1946, 1959, 1980 and 1992, to suit prevailing conditions. These essentially display a waxing and waning of revolutionary communism, climaxing in the 1980 constitution, which defined the country as 'a state of proletarian dictatorship' and the Communist Party as

SOCIAL INDICATORS

Life expectancy: 70
Infant mortality: 19 per 1000
Fertility rate, average per woman: 1.9
Literacy rate: adults 90.3 per cent
People per telephone: 87.8 per 1000 (including mobiles)
Internet users: 43 per 1000

'the vanguard and general staff of the Vietnamese working class'. More than a decade of hard-line communist rule failed to yield economic gains and the 1992 constitution reflected **reform** and a more open-door policy, including privatization of state-owned enterprises.

Government comprises a nominally elected 500-member National Assembly, a Council of State, a sort of collective presidency, and a Council of Ministers that manages governmental activities. Changes brought about by the **1992 constitution** gave enhanced powers to the National Assembly, previously little more than a rubber-stamp organization, while the presidency was once again invested in an individual. Nonetheless, effective political power remains in the hands of the Communist Party, primarily with the 15-member **Politburo**, the party's highest policy-making body. With ongoing political reforms a shift in emphasis is discernible and, for example, there is now greater inner-party **democracy**.

The economy of Vietnam suffered greatly from the disastrous imposition of orthodox Soviet-style central planning. Accordingly, the country remains one of the world's poorest, with a per capita income estimated at $550 per year.

With the collapse of the Soviet Union, failure of the economic model was recognized in 1986 with the government's adoption of the *doi moi* policy of renovation,

TRADE FIGURES

Vietnam's major export markets are the US, Japan, China, Australia, Singapore, Germany, and the UK. Exports to Asean countries increased by 28% in 2004 and to the EU by 24.4%. Export growth averaged 20% per year in the nineties with a growth leap of 31.5% in 2004 – representing 65% of GDP. By 2004 oil represented only 21% of exports, the industrial sector 56% of total export earnings. Encouraged by new company law that took effect in 2000, by 2005 (estimates), industry will contribute 40.9% services 38.1% and agriculture represent only 21% of GDP. Non-state industries reported 22.8% annual growth in 2004, exceeding the 7.1% growth of foreign-invested enterprises, and the 11% growth of State-owned enterprises. The Unified Law on Enterprise due for ratification in 2006 will eliminate discrimination between State-owned, foreign invested and private enterprises.

Above: *Business is brisk in Hue's colourful Dong Ba Market.*
Below: *Agricultural methods have changed little over the centuries.*

which resulted in continuing **reforms** and a gradual shift towards a market economy. In practice this has meant decollectivization and the rise of the private sector, along with **foreign investment**. Rallying from the adverse impact of the Asian economic crisis of 1997, Vietnam's GDP increased by 7.5per cent in 2004, third highest growth in Asia after Singapore and China.

Although manufacturing has increased rapidly since the mid-eighties, Vietnam remains an **agrarian** society, with agriculture and forestry occupying 63 per cent of the population but accounting for only 21 per cent of GDP. Rice is the major crop (Vietnam is the world's second-largest rice producer) though rice only represents 18.9 per cent of exports. Other economically important produce include coffee (Vietnam is now the world's second largest exporter of coffee after Brazil) as well as fish and seafood, rubber, tea, pepper, soybeans, cashew nuts, sugar cane, peanuts and bananas. It is the fourth largest exporter of footwear; the US is its largest export market. **Farming** is still mostly unmechanized and the water buffalo continues to be the driving force.

In 2003, oil represented 21 per cent of exports while three other product groups – garments and textiles, marine products and footwear – together produced 40 per cent of total export earnings. Seafood exports rose to $2.2 billion, an 8.8 per cent increase over 2002 placing Vietnam seventh in world seafood exporting nations.

Exports grew on average 20 per cent per annum in the nineties with a leap of 31.5 per cent in 2004 – 3.9 times higher than the GDP growth.

Rather surprisingly, Vietnam has added workers to its list of exports. As early as 2003, remittances from Vietnamese living overseas and expatriate workers, through official channels, amounted to a record $2.6 billion. In the year 2002, 46,122 Vietnamese workers went abroad and currently there are 420,000 Vietnamese working in Libya, S. Korea, Japan, Taiwan, and Malaysia and other countries.

Tourism in 2004, 2.9 million tourists visited Vietnam, the majority from Asian countries, the US, France and Australia.

THE PEOPLE

Vietnam's total **population** is estimated at 82.2 million and increasing at an annual rate of 1.3 per cent. About 63 per cent of the population is rural and concentrated in the two main rice-growing regions: the Red River Delta in the north and the Mekong Delta in the south. Population density is high, an average of 249 people per km^2 nationwide and more than 1,204 per km^2 in the Red River Delta (excluding Hanoi) – amongst the highest in the world for a rural region. In the larger Mekong Delta, home to more than 39.7 million people, population density is much lower at 430 per km^2.

The most populous cities are Ho Chi Minh City (Saigon) with a population of nearly 5.7 million people, Hanoi with a population of 3.1 million, and Haiphong with 1.8 million.

The vast majority of the people – some 86.2 per cent – are ethnic Vietnamese, the remainder made up of Chinese, Khmer, Cham and ethnic minorities. Vietnam possesses a complex ethnolinguistic mix within its 54 ethnic minorities.

The pattern of minority groupings is marked by a clear **ethnic** boundary in central northern Vietnam: to the north are mainly T'ai and Sinic minorities (T'ai, Tay and Muong tribespeople, among others), while to the south there are minorities belonging to the Malayo-Polynesian and Mon-Khmer language groups. The latter

Below: *An evocative sight – non la conical hats, woven from latania leaves, are traditional Vietnamese head coverings.*

includes the lowland Chams and the Lat of the Central Highlands as well as the Khmer Krom of the Mekong Delta.

Most interesting of the minorities are the highland peoples (termed *montagnards* by the French), who are tribal people who preserve their own distinct languages, customs and beliefs. Living mostly in the northern mountain areas and the Central Highlands, the hilltribes have been traditionally regarded by the Vietnamese (historically a lowland people) as hostile and uncivilized. Until modern times the minorities have been effectively autonomous, but the semi-**nomadic** lifestyles and the environmentally destructive slash-and-burn **agriculture** practised by some tribal groups have promoted the government to encourage settled communities.

YIN AND YANG

Using the I Ching (Book of Changes) as its reference, **Taoist** belief stresses a cosmic view based on two contrary yet complementary forces – *yin* (female) and *yang* (male). In order for **harmony** to be maintained in life, a proper balance has to be achieved between *yin* and *yang*. Imbalance between these forces is believed to be the root cause of illness.

Language

The official language is Vietnamese (kinh), the mother tongue of the vast majority of the population and it is also understood by many of the tribal minorities. The most widely spoken European languages are English, French, and to a far lesser degree, Russian.

Vietnamese is related to the Austroasiatic family of languages, but has had a complicated evolution, having been influenced by Mon-Khmer and T'ai and classical

Chinese. The first two influences provided the basic vocabulary, while T'ai brought Vietnamese its **tonal structure**. Chinese provided literary and technical terms and also the language's first written form, which used variations of Chinese characters until a romanized script was adopted in the early 20th century.

As a monosyllabic and tonal language, Vietnamese can be difficult for the Westerner. Six tones are used in the north, five in the south, and every syllable is inflected by a tone, which determines the meaning. Thus words sounding the same to the untrained ear may have five (or six) different meanings.

Religion

Vietnam is ostensibly a socialist country but religious practice is permitted by the 1980 constitution, which states 'citizens enjoy freedom of worship, and may practise or not practise a religion'. Historically, the spiritual life of the nation has been moulded by **Buddhism**, **Confucianism**, **Taoism** and **Animism**, the latter being the earliest and most deeply rooted belief of the ordinary people. Most people call themselves Buddhist, although their faith will in all likelihood incorporate Confucian, Taoist and Animistic beliefs along with orthodox Buddhist teaching. **Catholicism** has had a significant impact since colonial times, while **Islam** is practised by the small Cham minority. Besides major world religions, Vietnam also has its own home-grown faiths, the **Cao Dai** and **Hoa Hao** sects.

Above: *Dazzling saffron robes are worn by Buddhist monks at Da Nang.*
Opposite: *The goddess of mercy, Thien Nan, with many faces and arms to see and serve the needy, Phap Lam Pagoda, Da Nang.*
Below: *Religious ceremony in Ho Chi Minh City. Ritual offerings are made to appease malevolent spirits of divinities, and to revere benevolent ones.*

Buddhism

Mahayana Buddhism has always predominated in Vietnam, brought to the Red River Delta by Chinese monks in the late 2nd or early 3rd century AD. **Theravada Buddhism**, which historically had a stronghold in Sri Lanka

ARRIVAL OF CHRISTIANITY

The first Western missionaries set foot in north Vietnam in 1533, but it was not until 1615 that the first Christian missions were founded by Portuguese Jesuits in Hanoi, Da Nang and Hoi An. Many Vietnamese converted to Catholicism, which the ruling classes viewed as a threat to the traditional order of society. In the north, a decree forbidding the practice of Christianity was enforced between 1712 and 1720, while in the south foreign missionaries were expelled and the religion outlawed.

and later spread to Myanmar (Burma), Laos, Thailand and Cambodia, is practised in parts of Vietnam, especially in the Mekong Delta, where it is the faith of the Khmer Krom minority.

Confucianism and Taoism

A philosophy more than a religion, Confucianism was brought to Vietnam by the Chinese during their 1000-year domination of the country. It emphasizes **duty** and **moral obligation** in social relationships within the family and society, and takes its cardinal virtues as diligence, economy, integrity and righteousness. Confucian society is essentially hierarchical and based on virtue, which may be acquired through education.

In Vietnam, Confucianism was important among the mandarin class and in the past played an integral role in shaping government, bureaucracy and social order. Deep-rooted remnants remain in the Vietnamese respect for elders, for the birth order within the family and for education.

Right: *Ho Chi Minh City's red brick and granite Notre Dame Cathedral, located in the government quarter, was completed in 1883. It is said to occupy the site of an ancient pagoda.*

Another Chinese import, Taoism follows the mystical philosophy of Lao Tze, which expounds a highly complex system of correspondences, stressing basically the value of a contemplative and simple life in harmony with **nature**. Throughout Vietnam's feudal history, there has been a tradition of mandarins retreating to the mountains to become philosophers or poet monks.

Christianity

Catholicism was first brought to Vietnam by European **missionaries** in the16th century. It suffered persecution at times but succeeded in establishing a solid position under **French** rule. In modern times, the faith has suffered from its association with colonialism and with the 1950s administration of President Diem in South Vietnam. Converts today probably number as high as 10 per cent of the population.

The Protestant religion was introduced to Vietnam in the early 20th century. Today, Vietnamese Protestants number 200,000–300,000, although restrictions were imposed on religious activities after the war in 1975.

Islam and Hinduism

There are very small numbers of Muslims and Hindus in Vietnam, nearly all of them belong to the **Cham** minority. Hinduism was an important influence on the ancient Kingdom of Champa in central Vietnam, and while many Chams converted to Islam after the fall of their civilization, Hindu elements remained.

Cao Daism and Hoa Hao

Founded in 1919 by a Vietnamese mystic, Ngo Minh Chieu, the Cao Dai faith is an idealized religion embracing a mélange of beliefs derived principally from Mahayana Buddhism, Confucianism, Taoism and Christianity, as well as a lacing of spiritualism.

One of the basic tenets of the religion is that it is the 'third revelation', following two previous eras of 'missionary saints' – a list that embraces the founders of the world's major religions. **Cao Dai** thus claims to supersede

ANCESTOR WORSHIP

A part of the **Confucian** cultural tradition, ancestor worship pervades religious practice throughout Vietnam. Not only are ancestors revered, the souls of the dead are also believed to survive and act as a family's guardian spirits. **Ancestor shrines**, today typically featuring photographs of dead relatives, are commonly found in Vietnamese homes.

CAO DAISM

The doctrine was received by Ngo Minh Chieu as a series of revelations while he was living on Phu Quoc island in the Gulf of Thailand, off the west coast of the Mekong Delta. Headquarters were subsequently established at Tay Ninh, northwest of Ho Chi Minh City. Graham Greene described the religion in 1954: 'What on my first visit had seemed gay and bizarre was now like a game that had gone on too long.' Although it suffered persecution after the communist victory, **Cao Daism** survived and followers today are said to number about 2 million.

or correct misunderstanding in earlier teachings. There is also a belief in the soul and in an absolute supreme god. Coexisting with the supreme deity are lesser gods and numerous contactable spirits (including Shakespeare, Victor Hugo and Lenin).

Another indigenous religion, the **Hoa Hao** sect is almost exclusively associated with the Mekong Delta, where it was established in 1939. Its founder, Huynh Phu So – dubbed the 'Mad Monk' by the French – was born at Hoa Hao village, near Chau Doc. At the age of 20, he began preaching a personal version of Theravada Buddhism after the allegedly miraculous cure of a persistent illness.

With currently more than a million followers, the Hoa Hao faith stresses individual **prayer**, simplicity and social justice rather than elaborate rituals.

Art and Culture

Unlike its Southeast Asian neighbours, Vietnam has a culture heavily influenced by China rather than by the region's other great civilization, India. Accordingly, whereas the traditional art forms of Laos, Thailand and Cambodia share certain common elements, the arts and architecture of Vietnam stand in marked contrast.

This fundamental **cultural** distinction is compounded by **historical** factors. The Vietnamese have never been great builders, as were the ancient Khmers, for example. Moreover, such has been the country's turbulent past that few of the significant buildings have survived.

Ironically, while Vietnam's political and social history has been one of expansion and struggle for freedom from foreign domination, its art history reflects mostly the influence of imperial China. Vietnamese vernacular **architecture** has developed in temples, pagodas, palaces and imperial tombs, made from stone, brick and wood. Buildings can be impressive although most have generally been renovated and remodelled numerous times, with the result that period styles are not always easy to determine. Geomancy and concern for harmony in arrangement and positioning were important architectural considerations. In simple terms, **temples** and other major monuments tend to be squat, sturdy structures with thick, crusty roof tiles and a profusion of sculpted and carved ornamentation. The latter is often the most interesting aspect, and notably guardian spirits and other tutelary deities in painted or lacquered wood can be both beautiful and strikingly original. Nonetheless, the most distinctive classical art seen in Vietnam is not Vietnamese but that of the ancient Chams, who built tower-like religious monuments and produced some exquisite stone carving (best seen today in the **Museum of Cham Sculpture** at Da Nang).

Vietnam's decorative arts are highly developed, most obviously witnessed in temple decoration but also seen in traditional homes where carvings may adorn beams, partitions, windows and cornices – carpentry and carving are widespread skills. So, too, is the craft of making **lacquerware** (*son mai*), typically decorated with skilfully applied mother-of-pearl inlay.

Painting, both on canvas and on silk (a Vietnamese speciality), has in the past been a less accomplished art form than, for example, sculpture, in spite of silk painting dating back to the 13th century. In the modern age, however, painting has evolved remarkably and was given notable impetus during the French period. Social realism was the only acceptable art style under Ho Chi Minh, but with the greater freedoms of today, artists are able to exhibit work previously considered subversive, giving rise to a flourishing **contemporary art**, largely

Above Left: *Elaborate make-up and ceremonial costume in Chinese-influenced classical theatre.*
Opposite: *Chinese, Vietnamese and colonial features are blended in My Tho's Vinh Trang Pagoda.*
Below: *A student learns the importance of poise in Hanoi's school of dance.*

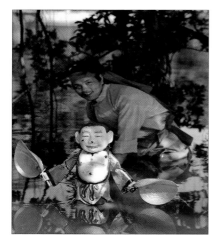

Western in form but Vietnamese in content, which is rapidly winning **international** acclaim.

Music and the **performing arts** have a long tradition in Vietnam and are closely allied in that theatre performances are always accompanied by an orchestra. Both have been heavily influenced by Chinese forms and, in the case of music, by Indian traditions via the Chams. Music and dance have also played an important part in both religious and court life. Vietnamese music has a five-tone scale and it is played on a variety of classical stringed instruments, flutes, drums and xylophones. Although complex, much is easily accessible, but some not easily appreciated by the untrained ear.

Classical theatre combines **music**, **poetry** (a highly developed art in Vietnam) and **drama**. Hat Tuong is akin to Chinese **opera**, while older Hat Cheo folk theatre is less formal and depends a good deal on improvization for its characteristic anti-establishment **satire**. The more modern form, *cai leung*, which employs elements of both *tuong* and *cheo* and has farcical overly-drawn characters, is quite easy to follow, without knowing a word of Vietnamese.

Above: *Carved from water resistant wood and painted in bright colours, water puppets may require as many as four people to operate them.* **Below:** *The day's catch is ferried to morning market. Seafood features strongly in Vietnamese cuisine.*

Water puppet theatre, unique to Vietnam, is highly entertaining and originated some 900 years ago as a folk art to accompany village festivals, when performances were staged on village ponds. This aquatic form of theatre features wooden puppets dextrously manipulated under water through bamboo rods, using a watery surface as the stage. Recently revived in Hanoi, water puppet shows based on peasant life and historical themes are performed daily.

Food and Drink

Although Chinese and French influences are discernible (French baguettes, for example), Vietnam has its own distinct **cuisine**, reputed to encompass more than 500 different dishes. **Rice** is the staple food and a typical meal comprises rice served from a communal bowl, eaten with helpings from other shared dishes of **pork**, **beef**, **chicken**, **vegetables**, **fish** and **seafood** (Vietnam's long coastline ensures abundant supplies). A soup is generally part of the menu and side servings of fresh raw green vegetables are also common. **Desserts** are typically sweet, such as sticky rice cakes and pastries, or fresh fruits.

The basic condiment is *nuoc mam*, a nutritious fermented fish sauce, a piquant flavouring and salt substitute. A spicier variation, *nuoc cham*, adds various ingredients such as chilli, lime juice, garlic and sugar to a base of *nuoc mam*. Other flavourings commonly used in Vietnamese cooking include lemon grass, basil, coriander and mint, as well as other spices typical of Southeast Asia. The food, however, is not especially spicy and while southern dishes tend to be hotter and make greater use of coconut milk than those in the north, many dishes are common to both regions.

Most typical of Vietnamese cuisine are **noodles** (*pho*), prepared as a soup with prawns, shredded beef or chicken. The Vietnamese eat noodles for breakfast, lunch or dinner – indeed, in villages, the traveller may find the dining choice limited to noodles. Another local favourite is spring rolls (*cha gio* in the south and *nem* in the north), fried thin rolls of rice paper stuffed with minced pork, prawn, crab meat, vermicelli, mushrooms and vegetables.

Drinks include **oriental tea** (usual with meals), strong coffee brewed from beans grown in the Central Highlands), imported and local **beer** (333 Export brand is a quite acceptable brew) and locally produced **wine** from Da Lat, which is quite palatable. Various local and imported soft drinks tend to be very sweet. Avoid drinking **tap water** or drinks containing ice.

Above: *Snakes are raised on farms and eating their flesh is believed to give men virile strength, so is drinking snake wine.*

READING THE MENU

fruit: *trai cay*
banana: *chuoi*
mango: *xoai*
coconut: *dua*
papaya: *du du*
bread: *banh mi*
coffee: *ca phe*
tea: *nuoc che*
beer: *bia*
mineral water: *nuoc suoi*
rice: *com trang*
vegetables: *rau xao*
(fried): (*hon hop*)
noodle soup: *pho*
beef: *bo*
chicken: *ga*
fish: *ca*
shrimp: *tom*

2
Hanoi

When Ly Thai Tho assumed power in the old capital, **Hoa Lu**, the way forward seemed clear: new dynasty – new capital. Guided by a heavenly vision, the first Ly emperor founded his new capital on a muddy alluvial plain in AD1010, creating first a royal enclosure, the Citadel, and then building city walls around it. The court drew in supporting craftsmen and the city grew. Throughout the next nine centuries, the court developed as a tight network of influential families whose scions rose as mandarins, constantly intriguing to seize power.

In spite of temporarily losing capital status to **Hue** during the 19th-century **Nguyen dynasty**, **Hanoi** is very much Vietnam's premier city. The French made it the administrative centre of their Indo-Chinese possessions, leaving behind a glorious architectural legacy in the city's many beautiful colonial villas and public buildings. North Vietnam was governed from here, and so is the reunified country today. For nearly half the country's 2000 years of history, Hanoi has provided the cultural force that has moulded the national character. As myths, legends and geomancy contributed much to the city's early planning, there is an appealing spirit of place about Hanoi.

Until fairly recently, Hanoi might have been considered a smaller, quieter, more traditional city than big and brash **Ho Chi Minh City** (Saigon). But in the past few years, Hanoi has rushed headlong into private enterprise and consumerism. New towers have shot skyward, new mini-towers (private homes and mini-hotels) have punctured the three-storey skyline and battalions of

DON'T MISS

*** Temple of Literature: visit a fascinating temple.
*** Old Quarter: explore and enjoy Hanoi's traditional urban scene.
*** Water Puppets: see an art form unique to Vietnam.
*** Fragrant Perfume Pagoda: see a beautiful fairytale rural setting.
*** Hanoi's new Museum of Ethnography: devoted to Vietnam's 54 minorities.
** Ho Chi Minh's Mausoleum: the memorial to Vietnam's modern architect.

Opposite: *Even in the Old Quarter, houses have added storeys and sprouted TV antennae.*

growling, bleeping motorbikes have replaced bicycles. Add now, a brand new shopping plaza complete with escalators – the first in Hanoi – just opened at one corner of Hoan Kiem Lake.

Yet despite the recent rapid changes, with its lakes, tree-lined boulevards, venerable pagodas and French colonial architecture, Hanoi remains a genuinely attractive city with its own distinct charm. The palaces of the **Citadel** may be long gone, but the **Old Town of 36 Streets** – the quarter originally occupied by the craftsmen who served the royal court – functions to this day, and not much has changed.

ORIENTATION

With a population of 3.5 million, Hanoi sits like a spider at the centre of its web in the midst of the Red River (Song Hong) Delta. Hanoi is primarily located on the left bank of the **Red River** some 70km (44 miles) from the coast. The Red River is spanned by two bridges, beyond which much new urban development continues well past the right bank.

Central Hanoi is divided into four administrative districts: **Hoan Kiem**, the heart of the city in the northeast quadrant; **Ba Dinh**, in the northwest, site of the ancient citadel; **Hai Ba Trung**, stretching along the river bank south of Hoan Kiem; and **Dong Da** in the southwest quadrant. Most sightseeing is concentrated in the first two districts.

HOAN KIEM DISTRICT AND OLD HANOI

Turning its back to the omnipotent river, its banks devoted to unattractive earthen flood dykes, the city focuses on **Hoan Kiem** (Lake of the Restored Sword), the undisputed heart of the city, lying southeast of where the old Citadel once stood. It is on the banks of Hoan Kiem Lake where Hanoians collectively wake up in the morning, stretch their legs, wave their wooden swords to the sound of a transistor, kick a shuttlecock or wind through a t'ai chi routine followed by a bit of gossip – all before half past seven.

Ngoc Son (Jade Mountain) Temple ★★

On an islet at the northern end of Hoan Kiem Lake, **Ngoc Son Temple** (open daily 08:00–17:00) is noted for its pretty,

Left: *The island temple of Ngoc Son is reached across an arched wooden bridge over Hoan Kiem Lake.*

tree-shaded location. Linked to the shore by a red wooden bridge named **The Huc**, which translates as the 'Flood of Morning Sunlight', the temple reputedly dates back to the **Tran dynasty** (1225–1400) and is dedicated to 13th-century national hero Tran Hung Dao – who saw off a 300,000 strong invasion dispatched by Kublai Khan in the 13th century – and two illustrious scholars of his time. The temple gate is flanked by huge Chinese characters representing Luck and Wealth. Beyond is a stone tower topped with a calligraphy paintbrush (**Thap But**, or 'Pen Tower') and next to it is the writing pad (**Dai Nghien**). The chunky, pagoda-style buildings on the island create a romantic impression and this temple, along with Tortoise Pagoda in the middle of Hoan Kiem Lake, are undoubtedly the most frequently portrayed symbols of Hanoi – they are shown every evening on national TV weather forecasts.

Old Town of 36 Streets ***
North of Hoan Kiem Lake lies the old artisans' and merchants' quarter, an area of crowded, narrow streets and tiny, huddled shophouses. It was established in the 13th century by Hanoi's 36 guilds, each in a different street and each street named after the guild's function. 'Hang' translates as merchandise, therefore **Pho Hang Gai** means 'Silk Street' – of great interest to contemporary shoppers. **Hang Bac** means 'Silver Street', which today includes gold as well as silver jewellery. There were guilds specializing in wooden and china bowls, in string instruments, sandals, baskets, leather, mats, sails, brushes, thread, bottles, herbal

MARKETS

Dong Xuan Market is an inveterate browser's dream. Lying north of Hoan Kiem Lake on Hang Khoa Street, this is Hanoi's largest general market with stalls selling all sorts of things, from food and flowers to clothes, household goods, live animals and traditional medicines. Although Vietnam's economic focus has now shifted more to the west, you may still find inexpensive Russian caviar and vodka.

medicine, incense, trays, hats, fans, coffins and bamboo. Among the most intriguing today are those devoted to red temple paraphernalia, votive papers (fake money for burning), tombstones and metal bashing – imagine listening to that din your entire life.

Den Bach Ma (White Horse Temple) ★

Located on Hang Buom Street in the Old Town, this well-preserved Taoist temple is dedicated to the spirit of **Bach Ma** (White Horse). It dates from the 9th century but has been repeatedly reconstructed, lastly in the 19th century. The story goes that the Ly Thai Tho, frustrated at his fruitless efforts to build the city walls (well, if you will build mud walls in a river flood plain), came here to pray. His prayers were answered when a white horse appeared from the temple and lead him to where he should build the walls. The only remainder of his walls is the **Old East Gate**, still standing at the end of **Pho Hang Chieu**, a few streets away.

Water Puppets ★★★

The **Municipal Water Puppet Theatre** stands at the northeast corner of **Hoan Kiem Lake** and no visitor to Hanoi should miss a performance of this irresistible art form, unique to Vietnam. Originally a folk art that began in village ponds as early as the 10th century, the light wooden figures are manipulated through long bamboo poles under water. They perform the most incredibly dextrous feats, drawing from scenes in history, mythology and village life, accompanied by traditional music and singing. There are performances daily (tel: 824 9494).

Cai Leung ★★

The **Cai Leung Theatre** in the old town stages what might be termed **Vietnamese musicals** – no Vietnamese necessary. *Cai leung* is an amalgam of ***cheo***, the earliest form of folk mime and spoken drama. Plots, set in feudal days, are often

HANOI HILTON

With gallows humour US prisoners of war dubbed **Hoa Lo Prison** the Hanoi Hilton. Sections inside the forbidding walls were also euphemistically named – Heartbreak Hotel, for example, described the solitary confinement cells measuring 1.8m x 1.8m (6ft x 6ft). Built by the French in the early 20th century, the site, in Hoa Lo Street, has been redeveloped with a complex that includes, ironically, a luxury hotel.

HANOI'S ORIGINS

In AD1010, as legend has it, **Ly Thai Tho** was seeking the site of a new capital. While cruising the Red River, he saw a dragon preparing to take wing – an auspicious sign. So, on this spot, Ly Thai Tho built Thang Long – the Soaring Dragon – now Southeast Asia's oldest surviving capital. Over the centuries the name changed, to **Dong Kinh** (from which the Europeans derived their name for northern Vietnam, **Tonkin**), and finally, in 1831, to **Ha Noi** (City by the River).

Left: *The grim exterior of the former 'Hanoi Hilton' prison no longer inspires fear.*

HANOI MUSEUMS

Highly recommended museums (usually closed for two-hour lunches and on Mondays) include:

History Museum, 1 Pho Pham Ngu Lao Street, a beautiful building holding a fine, vast collection of artefacts from all periods of Vietnam's past.

Museum of Ethnography, Van Huyen Street, Hanoi's newest museum, well worth the 7km (4 mile) trek to see a vast collection of artefacts and costumes of the 54 ethnic minorities.

Womens' Museum, 36 Pho Ly Thuong Kiet, inevitably patriotic, but also holding a collection of minority traditional costumes.

Ho Chi Minh Museum, Bao Tang Ho Chi Minh, documentation and memorabilia of the country's founding father.

comic to the point of farce with clearly recognizable heroes and villains, irreverently poking fun at feudal officials. One of the most beautiful, poignant and funny, is a dramatization of Vietnam's epic poem, 'Kieu', composed by poet Nguyen Du (1765–1820). The costumes are colourful and wildly extravagant, the traditional music a delightful challenge to the ear. Saturday and Sunday nights at 8pm (72 Hang Bac Street, tel: 825 7823).

BA DINH DISTRICT AND THE WEST LAKE

Immediately west of the Old Town is the huge open space once occupied by the Citadel. This was the site of the **Imperial Palace** of the late **Le dynasty**, mostly destroyed in the 17th century. Later fortifications built on the same site have similarly vanished except for the North Gate on Phan Dinh Phung Street and the hexagonal Flag Tower (Cot Co) on Dien Bien Phu Street, built in 1812 and now a Hanoi landmark.

Further northwest lies the southern shore of **West Lake** (Ho Tay) which at 583ha (1440 acres), is Hanoi's largest lake, separated by a narrow causeway (Thanh Nien Street) from the smaller **White Silk Lake** (Ho Truc Bach). The creation of Ho Tay is credited variously to a stampeding golden buffalo calf or a dragon-king.

LOTUS SYMBOL

Rising above the water on its single column the One Pillar Pagoda represents a lotus flower. The flower is a Buddhist symbol; just as the lotus has its roots buried in mud under water, yet manages to rise above the surface and open its flower in the sunlight, so the Buddha was born in the impure world but through his Enlightenment he rose above it.

Tran Quoc and Quan Thanh Pagodas **

One of Hanoi's oldest temples, **Tran Quoc** Pagoda was originally built on the banks of the Red River but moved in the 17th century to its present site beside the causeway on West Lake's southeastern shore. A stele dated 1639 records the temple's history. At the southern end of the causeway, **Quan Thanh** is a typically ornate temple honouring Tran Vo, guardian spirit of the north. Noted for its large bronze bell, cast in 1677, and its towering bronze statue of Tran Vo, the temple originally dates from the 11th or 12th century, during the Le dynasty, although it has subsequently been reconstructed twice.

One Pillar Pagoda (Chua Mot Cot) ***

Elegantly raised on a single column above a pond and designed to represent a lotus emerging from the water, this charming little wooden pagoda is near Ho Chi Minh's Mausoleum. It was originally built in the 11th century by **Emperor Ly Thai Tho** who, lacking an heir, dreamt he was presented with a male child seated on a lotus flower by **Quan An**, the Goddess of Mercy. A short while later, the emperor married a peasant girl who gave birth to a son and heir. In gratitude Ly Thai Tho built the **One Pillar Pagoda**. This highly revered shrine has been rebuilt several times, most notably in the fifties after it was torched by the French during their final retreat from Hanoi in 1954. The nearby Bo tree was a gift from India, planted in 1958. In the same compound is the pretty little **Dien Huu Pagoda**.

Above: *Rising out of its lotus pond, the One Pillar Pagoda is one of the delights of Hanoi.*
Opposite: *In a peaceful spot overlooking the West Lake, Tran Quoc's name translates as 'Defence of the Country'.*

Temple of Literature (Van Mieu) ***

Open daily (08:30–11:30 and 13:30–16:30) except on Mondays. This is Hanoi's most impressive temple, notable for its **historical** importance, **architectural** interest and, not least, **meditative atmosphere**. Located in an extensive compound south of the Citadel, between Nguyen Thai Hoc and Quoc Tu Giam streets, the **Temple of Literature** was founded in 1070 by Emperor Le Thanh Tong and dedicated to **Confucius**. Six years later it became the national **university** (Quoc Tu Giam), established to teach the children of royalty and the aristocracy (mandarins). The

HO CHI MINH'S MAUSOLEUM

Directly south of the Presidential Palace is the unmistakable grey marble mausoleum where Ho Chi Minh's mortal remains are preserved in a glass casket. The imposing, but stark, building was constructed between 1973 and 1975. Open on Tuesdays, Wednesdays, Thursdays and Saturdays from 08:00 to 11:00 and on Sundays from 07:30 to 11:30.

Right: *Roll of honour – successful scholars had to endure over 30 days of doctoral examinations before graduating as mandarins.*

long, narrow temple compound, pleasantly planted with banyan and frangipani, is divided into five walled courtyards and, despite repeated renovations, the various halls and pavilions remain fine examples of traditional architecture. The main entrance is on the south side (Quoc Tu Giam St), and beyond the first courtyard is Khue Van Cac (Pavilion Dedicated to the Constellation of Literature). In the next compound is Thien Quang Tinh (Well of Heavenly Clarity), and flanking this large pool is the temple's most famous sight – 82 stone stelae resting on the backs of stone tortoises, inscribed with the names and places of birth of successful candidates in the doctoral examinations held here between 1442 and 1780. Another gate leads to the **Great House of Ceremonies**, where a colossal red statue of **Confucius** reigns.

Presidential Palace *

This early 20th-century French colonial building on Hung Vuong Street was formerly the residence of the Governor-General of Indo-China and is today used for state functions. Reputedly, Ho Chi Minh refused to live here.

SOUTHEAST OF HOAN KIEM LAKE

South of Hoan Kiem Lake is the former French quarter

TRADITIONAL MUSIC

Vietnam's delightful music played on **traditional** musical instruments – the one-stringed monochord (dan bau), the 16-stringed zither (dan tranh), a long-necked, moon-shaped guitar (nguyet), a pear-shaped lute (dan ty ba), drums, bamboo flutes, and upright bamboo xylophones – can often be heard at the **Temple of Literature**, upstairs at the **Ho Chi Minh Museum**, at the **Water Puppet** and **Cai Leung Theatres** and in certain restaurants.

where the landscape changes to one of broad, leafy boulevards and ochre Paris-style villas, the best of which are now occupied by embassies and government offices.

Opera House ★★★
At the east end of Trang Tien Street, this grand building, completely renovated in 1997, stands as a golden jewel of French colonial culture. A replica of the magnificent Paris Opera built in 1911, it is now less romantically known as the Municipal Theatre. See local newspapers for current performances.

St Joseph's Cathedral (Nha Tho Lon) ★
Situated on Ly Quoc Su Street, the cathedral was consecrated in 1886. With its twin-tower, neo-Gothic façade and stained-glass windows, it is a startling reminder of European influence. Masses are held daily from 05:00 to 07:00 and from 17:00 to 19:00. At other times the doors may be locked. Visitors should enquire at the nearby Diocese of Hanoi on Nha Chung Street.

Ba Da Pagoda ★
Further down the street and across the road from St Joseph's is **Ba Da Pagoda** (Heavenly Mistress of the Stone), a Buddhist temple dating from the 15th century. It is easily

FINE ARTS MUSEUM

A short walk away from the Temple of Literature is the Fine Arts Museum at 66 Nguyen Thai Hoc Street. The museum, contained in an exotic **colonial building** with an **oriental roof**, has an extensive collection of **artefacts** covering some of Vietnam's ethnic minorities and prehistory. Exhibits include sculpture, painting and lacquerware and examples of ancient and contemporary Vietnamese art. Somewhat heavy on propaganda, the museum is open from Tuesday to Sunday (08:00–12:00 and 13:00–16:00).

HO CHI MINH'S STILT HOUSE

Virtually behind Ho Chi Minh's **Mausoleum** is the wooden stilt house (**Nha San Bac Ho**) built for him by the nation. It is where he lived from 1958 until his death in 1969. The house is constructed like a peasant's home and is now open as a museum, set in pretty landscaped gardens.

Left: *The elegant renovated exterior of the French Opera House, now rather unromantically called the Municipal Theatre.*

overlooked because of its uninspiring exterior, but the interior is surprisingly interesting for its clutter of religious objects and gilt statues of Buddha.

The temple derives its name from a stone statue reputed to have magical properties. The original has since been lost and a wooden replica stands in its place.

Chua Quan Su (Ambassadors' Pagoda) **

Southwest of Hoan Kiem, on Quan Su Street, this temple was completed in 1942. It is notable for occupying the site of a 17th-century reception house for visiting **Buddhist** ambassadors and envoys from other Buddhist countries.

DAY EXCURSIONS FROM HANOI
Chua Huong Tich (Fragrant Perfume Pagoda) ***

The site of an annual Buddhist pilgrimage (during March and April), this is a series of shrines set in grottoes in the limestone cliffs of Huong Tich Son (Mountain of the Fragrant Traces), 70km (43 miles) southwest of Hanoi. Dating mostly from the 17th century, the pagoda grottoes have evocative names: among others, **Pagoda Leading to Heaven** (Thiem Chua) and **Purgatory Pagoda** (Giai Oan Chua). The site is approached by road, then enchantingly by boat poled along the Yen River. The landscape of limestone mountains and

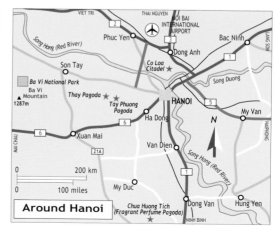

Around Hanoi

green paddy fields makes this one of the most stunning rural scenes in the whole of North Vietnam. (*See* Tam Coc and Hoa Lu, Chapter 3).

Co Loa *

The site of Vietnam's very first capital is located in rural Dong Anh district, 15km (9 miles) northwest of Hanoi. Little remains of the once extensive snail-shaped ramparts of the fortified Citadel founded in 255BC, although modern excavations reveal sufficient examples. A temple is dedicated to Emperor An Duong who was defeated by the Chinese when his daughter, married to the son of a Chinese general, revealed the secret of her father's magic crossbow to her husband, thus beginning a thousand years of Chinese domination. A traditional communal house (*dinh*) and a small museum add to the interest. Not monumental, but enough for history enthusiasts.

Thay and Tay Phuong Pagodas ***

Both these pagodas, situated some 40km (25 miles) south-west of Hanoi in Ha Son Binh Province, are well worth visiting for their intrinsic interest and lovely settings.

Located at Sai Son Village, **Thay Pagoda** (Pagoda of the Master), officially named Thien Phuc (Heavenly Blessing), dates from the 12th century and is dedicated to Emperor Le Than Tong and Tu Dao Hanh, a monk renowned as an herbalist and a water puppeteer – hence the epithet 'master'. In addition to the temple, the site is notable for its traditional water puppet theatre and the Sai Son hill, whose caves can be explored.

On the seventh day of the third lunar month, the Thay Pagoda Festival provides an excellent opportunity for visitors to watch traditional water puppet theatre in a village setting on the artificial lake said to have been created by Tu Dao Hanh.

Nearby is the hilltop **Tay Phuong Pagoda** (West Pagoda), reached by a flight of some 250 steps. Designed as three buildings with most distinctive roofs, the originally 8th-century pagoda houses many excellent examples of traditional Vietnamese wood sculpture.

Above: *Goods on their way to market in time-honoured tradition.*

HANDICRAFT VILLAGES

In addition to the craft guilds of the Old Town, numerous craft villages supplied the royal court at the Citadel. **Bat Trang**, 13km (8 miles) southeast, is still producing fine ceramics; **Van Phuc**, 8km (5 miles) southwest, is still weaving silk for domestic and export markets; **So**, 25km (15 miles) southeast, is noted for its noodles and **Dong Ky**, 15km (9 miles) northeast, has diversified from producing firecrackers – now banned – to producing inlaid mother-of-pearl furniture.

Hanoi at a Glance

BEST TIMES TO VISIT

Autumn (**Oct–Nov**) or spring (**Apr–Jul**) are the most pleasant months when the weather is cool and sunny.

GETTING THERE

Hanoi's sleek new **Noi Bai International Airport** is 35km (22 miles) from the city – the journey takes about 1hr. In **Hanoi** there is a choice between the slightly more expensive metered airport **taxis**, ordinary metered city taxis and a cheap, convenient airport mini-bus, which for a small extra cost, will drop you at your hotel.
International **trains** run from Hanoi to Nanning and Kunming.

GETTING AROUND

Taxis cruise the streets and can be booked by telephone or found near hotels. **Taxi** operators include: City Taxi, tel: (4) 822 222; Red Taxi, tel: (4) 856 8686. Self-drive **hire cars** are not available. Hiring a **car and driver** at a daily rate is relatively inexpensive for longer journeys. Tourist cafés offer cheap **day trips** to many tourist sites including **Ha Long Bay**. Short distances in town are most easily covered by taxi, *cyclo* (pedicabs) or *xe oms* (motorbike taxis). Hanoi's public buses are impractical for the visitor. Sightseeing is best done **walking** or, for the intrepid in view of Hanoi's traffic, by **bicycle**. Bikes can be rented.

WHERE TO STAY

Hanoi now boasts ten hotels of international standard.

LUXURY

Sofitel Metropole Hanoi, 15 Ngo Quyen Street, tel: (4) 826 6919, fax: (4) 826 6920, e-mail: sofitelhanoi@hn.vnn.vn
Hilton Hanoi Opera, 1 Le Thanh Tong Street, tel: (4) 933 0500, fax: (4) 933 0530, e-mail: hanoi@hilton.com This huge monument to modernity was opened in 1999 beside the Opera House.
Melia Hanoi, 44 Ly Thuong Kiet Street, tel/fax: (4) 934 3343, website: www.melia hanoi.com Even more sumptuous, built on the site of the prison; dubbed the 'Hanoi Hilton' by US prisoners of the Vietnam War.
Sunway, 19 Pham Dinh Ho Street, tel: (4) 971 3888, fax: (4) 971 3555, e-mail: sunway hnresv@fpt.vn www.sunway-hotel.com Only hotel in Hanoi with potable tap water and triple-glazed windows.
Hanoi Horison, 40 Cat Linh Street, a few streets west of Hoan Kiem Lake, tel: (4) 733 0808, fax: (4) 733 0688, e-mail: Sales@hanoihorison hotel.com.vn The service is Împeccable at this five-star Swiss-Belhotel.

MID-RANGE

Guoman Hanoi (four-stars), 83A Ly Thuong Kiet Street, tel: (4) 822 2800, fax: (4) 822 2822, web: www.guoman hotels.com Good rooms a few streets from Hoan Kiem Lake.
Galaxy Hotel (three-stars), 1 Phan Dinh Phung Street, tel: (4) 828 2888, fax: (4) 828 2466, e-mail: Galaxyhtl@vnn.vn

BUDGET

Dan Chu Tourist, 29 Trang Tien Street, tel: (4) 825 4937, fax: (4) 826 6786, e-mail: danchutourist@vnn.vn A well-run government owned hotel near the Metropole and Hanoi Opera.
Army Hotel, 33C Pham Ngu Lao, tel: (4) 825 2896, fax: (4) 826 5541, e-mail: armyhotel @fpt.vn Another huge government run hotel, near Hoan Kiem Lake, with a pool.

WHERE TO EAT

Hanoi restaurants now run close competition with those of Ho Chi Minh City, for creative menus and appealing decor.

LUXURY

Emperor, 18b Le Thanh Tong Street, tel: (4) 826 8801. Elegant villa that offers excellent food and moderate prices.
Club Opera, 59 Ly Thai To Street, tel: (4) 824 6950. Cosy, chic atmosphere across from the Sofitel, mid-price.
Bobby Chin Restaurant, 1 Ba Trieu Street, on the south side of Hoan Kiem Lake, tel: (4) 934 8577, email: Info@ bobbychinn.com www. bobbychinn.com Offers true fusion food – American-Chinese-Egyptian chef.

MID-RANGE

Brother's Café, 26 Nguyen Thai Hoc Street, tel: (4) 733 3866. *The* place to try everything that's Vietnamese! An inexpensive buffet lunch and good, reasonably-priced barbecue dinner in an old merchant's house.

Indochine, 16 Nam Ngu, tel: (4) 942 4097. A vast Vietnamese menu, try prawns steamed in a coconut shell.

Hoa Sua, 81 Tho Nhuon, tel: (4) 942 4448. Visit the terrace behind the villa and try the French or Vietnamese food to help the street children, who train here as chefs and waiters.

SHOPPING

Hanoi is good for silk – try 'silk street', **Hang Gai** – in the old town. Other good buys are gold jewellery, jade, amber, lacquer, ceramics, embroidered **T-shirts**, **brocade**, **sculpture**, **paintings** and **antiques** (check if export is permitted; customs confiscate items on departure). For paintings, check the galleries along **Pho Trang Tien**, **Hang Gai** and, its extension, **Hang Bong Street.** For Vietnam's top **artists**, contact Suzanne Lecht's gallery, ART VIETNAM, 30 Hang Than Street, tel: (4) 844 9272 349, fax: (4) 844 9272 804, e-mail: artvietnam@fpt.vn www.vietnamesefineart.com who arranges exhibitions abroad. For **jewellery**, compare the shops along **Hang Bac Street**. For books about Vietnam in English, French and

Vietnamese, contact **The Gioi Publishers** at 46 Tran Hung Dao Street, tel: (4) 934 3196, fax: (4) 825 3841, e-mail: thegioi@hn.vnn.vn

TOURS AND EXCURSIONS

Hanoi has been besieged by tour operators engaged in cutthroat competition. Top end gets you a car and a driver, in the mid-range a minibus and at the bottom end, a very full bus.

LUXURY

Vidotour, 8 Thien Quang Street, Hai Ba Trung District, tel: (4) 942 8290, fax: (4) 942 8295, e-mail: hanoi@vidotourtravel.com www.vidotourtravel.com This operator specializes in 'hand-made tours'.

MID-RANGE

Handspan Adventure Travel, F9 Sun Red River Blvd, 23 Phan Chu Trinh, booking office 80 Ma May, tel: (4) 933 2377, fax: (4) 933 2378, e-mail: handspan@hn.vnn.vn **Sapa Tours-Pacific Travel**, 30 Hang Be, tel: (4) 836 4212, fax: (4) 856 7862, email: info@sapatours.com www.bamboosapahotel.com

BUDGET

Vietnamopentour-Sinhcafe, 30 Hang Be Street, tel: (4) 836 4212/756 8868, fax: (4) 756 7862, e-mail sinhcafe@hn. vnn.vn www.sinhcafe.com

USEFUL CONTACTS

International Hospital, Benh Vien Bach Mai, tel: (4) 574 0740, 24-hour emergencies; Gia Phong, tel: (4) 547 1111.

Hanoi Family Medical Practice, Van Phuc Compound, 298 I Kim Ma Road, Ba Dinh District, Hanoi, tel: 24hr hotline (4) 843 0748 or Japanese (8) 822 1919, e-mail: rafi@vietnammedicalpractice. com www.vietnammedical practice.com

The Dental Clinic, Van Phuc Compound, 298 I Kim Ma Road, Ba Dinh District, Hanoi, tel: (4) 823 0281.

Viet Duc Hospital, Benh Vien Viet Duc, 40 Pho Trang Thi, tel: (4) 825 3531. Open 24hr.

International SOS Clinic, 31 Hai Ba Truung Street, tel: (4) 934 0555, fax: (4) 934 0556.

Vietnam Airlines, 94 Pho Quang Trung, tel: (4) 832 0320, email: glp.mkpl@ vietnamair.com.vn www.vietnamairlines.com

HANOI	J	F	M	A	M	J	J	A	S	O	N	D
AVERAGE TEMP. °F	61	62	68	74	81	83	84	82	80	76	70	64
AVERAGE TEMP. °C	16	17	20	23	27	29	29	28	27	25	21	18
HOURS OF SUN DAILY	2	1	2	3	6	5	6	5	5	6	4	4
RAINFALL in	1	1	2	3	8	10	13	14	10	4	2	1
RAINFALL mm	18	26	44	90	188	240	288	318	265	130	43	24
DAYS OF RAINFALL	8	11	15	13	14	15	16	17	14	9	7	6

3
The North

It is easy to think of Hanoi as being at the very top of Vietnam, although in fact a considerable expanse of territory stretches north and west from the capital to the Chinese and Laotian borders. This highland region is Vietnam's historic heartland, the land fought over by the early Viets and the Chinese. It is attractive for its extraordinary mountainous landscapes (some of the finest in the country) and its rich assortment of hill tribe minorities, including the Dao, H'mong, Coin, Man, Lu, Tay, Nung, Black and White T'ai, and Muong, each with its distinctive sartorial style.

The North, as referred to by the Vietnamese, extends south from the Chinese border to just above the city of Hue – the 17th parallel was the former division between North and South Vietnam. In outline, the region is shaped like a club, the rounded 'head' at the top comprising mountains and the delta plains of the **Red River**, the 'handle' at the bottom formed by a narrow coastal plain backed by the northern span of the **Truong Son** mountain range.

However, it should be remembered that the area has only recently been added to the travel map, and tourism facilities in some areas are comparatively sparse.

Apart from short day trips, essentially there are three recommended excursion options from Hanoi: a journey east to Ha Long Bay and Cat Ba Island National Park; a journey north to Sa Pa to visit the minority ***montagnard*** tribes and a journey northeast to visit Ba Be Lakes as well as hill tribes.

DON'T MISS

*** Ha Long Bay: behold a haunting seascape.
** Cat Ba National Park: view a rich variety of flora, fauna and good beaches.
** Sa Pa: see spectacular mountain scenery and minority hill people.
** Ba Be Lakes: witness more stunning scenery and minority hill tribes.
* Dien Bien Phu: visit the site of calamitous French defeat in a remote valley setting.

Opposite: *A typical northern landscape in lush Hoa Binh Province.*

EXPLORING THE NORTH

The most convenient way to make an excursion into the mountainous north is by hiring a car or 4-wheel-drive **vehicle** and a **driver** in Hanoi. However, Hanoi travel agencies and tourist cafés have made it easy with a wide variety of tours, some for adventurous trekkers, others for sedentary observers. Roads to the main centres have improved, but remain poor – or non-existent – in remote areas. Alternatively, there are **rail** links between **Hanoi** and **Lao Cai** (12hr), which is the nearest rail point for **Sa Pa**, and northeast to **Lang Son** (6hr) on the Chinese border, from which there are buses.

EAST OF HANOI
Ha Long Bay ★★★

Spectacular **Ha Long Bay** with its mysterious limestone karsts erupting abruptly from the jade green sea has quite justifiably been named a World Heritage Site by UNESCO. At any time of year, even during the mists of winter, this landscape is beguiling, constantly changing as your boat edges closer, weaving amongst the labyrinth of this colossal green maze.

Ha Long Bay is an archipelago of some 3000 islands, both huge and miniscule, belonging to the coastal province of **Quang Ninh** and covering about 1500km² (579 square miles).

The name Ha Long translates to 'where the dragon descends into the sea'. A local legend relates how this seascape was created when a giant dragon dashed down from the mountains to the coast, its footprints gouging the upturned karsts as it plunged into the sea. A number of caves and grottoes, some illuminated, can be visited, the finest being the huge Hang Dau Go Cave which, with its superb stalactites and stalagmites, was appropriately named *Grotte des Merveilles* (Grotto of Wonders) by the French. Some caves have yielded artefacts confirming that humanity has inhabited these regions for 6000 years.

Ha Long City, 160km (101 miles) east of Hanoi on a splendid new motorway, lies divided by the bay, with **Bai Chay** on the south bank and **Hon Gai** on the north. Most

Opposite Top: *Ha Long Bay has some spectacular caves and grottoes, many of which can be visited by boat from Haiphong and Hon Gai.*
Opposite Bottom: *In the Red River Delta the prime money-earner is rice.*
Right: *Ha Long Bay, a watery green maze that seems to go on forever.*

hotels and restaurants are in Bai Chay. Although Bai Chay lies on a long, wide beach, it is muddy and not particularly appealing. Also, in recent years Ha Long City has turned itself into a 'pleasure centre' for Hanoians and even the Chinese, who come south seeking 'Thai massage' – a euphemism for prostitution.

Particularly in the popular summer months, there is no real reason to stay in Ha Long Bay other than to catch a boat for a tour through the islands. The easy option is to book a tour from Hanoi that includes the bus, hotel, meals and sometimes a night aboard a comfortable boat en route to **Cat Ba Island**.

Haiphong

Located on the right bank of the **Cam River** and supporting a population of 1.6 million in the greater metropolitan area, Haiphong was largely created by the French in the late 19th century. What had been a small harbour was then transformed into a commercial centre and port designed to rival Hong Kong.

Historically, the city is best known for a tragic incident that sparked the First **Indo-China War**. In 1946, when tension was running high between France and Vietnam, the French bombarded **Haiphong** and inflicted huge casualties on the civilian population. A few weeks later war broke out. The city suffered further bombing during the Second Indo-China War. In the last few years there has been much rebuilding and new industrial expansion.

CLIMATE

Best months to visit this area are from **March** to **May** and **September** to **December**. The summer, from April to September, is very hot and humid, with sporadic outbursts of heavy rain. Northern Vietnam is very cold and wet between December and March.

Although **Haiphong** has been ravaged by latter-day development, a certain amount of colonial architecture survives, and ports tend to have a fascination of their own. For most visitors a half-day's sightseeing is sufficient. Among the city's most ornate buildings, the 300-year-old **Du Hang Pagoda** is a notable example of traditional Vietnamese architecture, and the Hang Kenh Communal House, (once a community centre and temple), has a remarkable collection of 500 wood carvings.

Situated halfway up **Elephant Mount**, on a rocky hill on the outskirts of Haiphong, the **Chi Lai Communal House** has been converted into a museum displaying Neolithic bronzes. The caves on the mount were used as a guerrilla base during the war with the French. In the war with the USA, there was an anti-aircraft battery where female gunners reputedly downed US fighter planes. Alternatively, should you find yourself in Haiphong with an afternoon between flight and hydrofoil, visit Do Son beach resort (first developed by the French and still popular with Hanoians and expats), located on a long hilly promontory some 20km (12 miles) southeast of Haiphong. The 4km (2.5 miles) long promontory ends in a string of islets. Apart from the beach, Do Son is also the site of the first – and only – casino in Vietnam (established in 1975). It is open to foreigners only.

Cat Ba Island **

Lying about 30km (19 miles) from Ha Long City, a fast (45-minute), or slow (4-hour), boat ride away, this large inhabited island covers an area of 354km² (137 square miles). About half of it is protected as a national park. Characterized by spectacular 300m (985ft) limestone cliffs, the island was once a pirate haunt but is now noted for its surprising range of **natural habitats** – tropical evergreen forest, freshwater lake, mangrove, sandy shore and coral reef – supporting a rich variety of wildlife, including monkeys, deer, gibbons, wild boar and hornbills. The island offers an attractive mix of forested hills, waterfalls and caves, as well as beaches and a busy waterfront scene in **Cat Ba Town**.

NORTH OF HANOI
Sa Pa **

Those with more time might take a bus or a (12-hour) train to Lao Cai, the border town and railhead for **Sa Pa**, now fully reconstructed after being destroyed by the Chinese in 1979. There are daily markets but the big market in Sa Pa is on Sunday where **Black H'mong** and **Red Dao** push their wares rather aggressively.

Although Vietnam's highest mountain peak, **Fansipan**, standing at 3143m (10,215ft), can be seen from Sa Pa on a clear day, it can only be reached on foot and the trip with a guide takes at least three days. There are no huts or facilities; self-sufficient camping gear and food must be carried.

Opposite: *Characteristic minority architecture near Sa Pa. At high altitudes, where there is little risk of flooding, homes do not need to be raised on stilts.*

KIEP BAC PAGODA

Tran Hung Dao is revered as a kind of guardian spirit. A temple in his honour, dating from the 13th century, is located 61km (38 miles) from Hanoi, 15km (9 miles) north of Hai Dong, en route to Ha Long Bay. A popular annual festival is held at the temple on the anniversary of his death on the 20th of the 8th lunar month (September/October).

The North

From Sa Pa, a four-wheel-drive vehicle is necessary to
get to **Bac Ha** (Sunday market) to see **Flower H'mong** and
Dao minorities, or from Bac Ha to Can Cau (Saturday
market) in the mountains of the Flower H'mong people. A
much smaller market in the mountains at **Can Cau** can be
reached over a bumpy road, slowly, with a normal car.

A northwest loop from Sa Pa might include the two
markets at **Binh Lu** and **Cam Duong** (Flowering H'mong,
Dao, Tien, Coin, Man and Lu) then on to Lai Chau,
passing through remote, forested highlands of stunning
beauty, then south to the battlefield of Dien Bien Phu near
the Laos border, where the French were decisively defeated
by the **Viet Minh** in 1954. A small museum, along with a
reconstruction of the French command post and a few
other reminders of the battle, can be seen at the site. There
are separate monuments honouring the Viet Minh and the
French who died. The attractive valley and surrounding
mountains evoke a tingling sensation of remoteness, while
scattered in the hills are villages of Thai and other minority
groups. At **Cam Duong** over-night home stays can be
arranged (a permit is required) with minority peoples.

Ba Be Lake **

From Hanoi, a northeast
loop aiming for Ba Be Lake
– actually three lakes
linked together, fed by
the Nang River – would
pause at the town of
Thai Nguyen to visit the
Museum of Ethnography,
pass through Bac Can and
arrive at Ba Be Lake in the
evening. After sleeping in
the village of **Cho Ra** on
the lake shore, a boat takes
you to visit Puong Cave en
route to Pac Ngoi village
(Tay and Nung people) on
the far side of the lake. This

is followed by a walk to **Dau Dang Waterfall** which offers breathtaking scenery and the opportunity to visit hill people at **Pac Ngoi** village before returning to **Bac Can**. From here one would travel north to **Cao Bang** near the Chinese border to see **Ban Doc Waterfall** and then south again via Lang Son (Nhi Thanh and Tam Thanh caves), to Hanoi.

SOUTH OF HANOI
Mai Chau
En route to Sa Pa, Mai Chau, 135km (73 miles) southwest of Hanoi is the nearest place to see minority people in a sprinkling of rural hamlets on a day excursion from Hanoi. Overnight stays in a **White Thai** stilt house can be arranged, also treks to a Lac village (Ban Lac) and a H'mong village (Xa Linh).

Hoa Lu and Tam Coc **
Attractively sited in a mountain setting at the village of **Truong Yen**, 102km (65 miles) south of Hanoi, **Hoa Lu** was an Imperial City during the pre-Hanoi Dinh (968-80) and Early Le (980-1009) dynasties. The entire former capital lies destroyed beneath the rice paddies, although archaeological investigation has revealed much of historical and artistic interest. The only sites remaining of the Citadel are two temples, **Dinh Tien Hoang**, temple of the Dinh emperors, and **Dai Hanh**, temple of the Early Le emperors.

Known as 'Ha Long Bay of the rice paddies', a watery plain, from which huge limestone karsts rear up abruptly resembling those in Guilin and Yangshuo in China, is

Left: *Valley-dwelling minorities eke out a living by farming and rearing livestock such as chickens, ducks and pigs.*
Opposite: *Minority tribespeople of the northern uplands practise shifting cultivation and lead a migratory lifestyle.*

CUC PHUONG NATIONAL PARK

Located west of Nam Dinh, 140km (87 miles) from Hanoi, Cuc Phuong is one of Vietnam's few national parks, established in 1962. An area of primary tropical forest, the preserve extends over 25,000ha (61,728 acres) and shelters an immensely varied list of flora (nearly 2000 species) and fauna (animals, 64 species; reptiles, 33; birds, 137). Caves in the limestone mountains have yielded prehistoric finds.

Right: *A typical mode of
transport on Highway 1,
which runs virtually the
full length of Vietnam.*

HIGHWAY 1

One of the longest and most
famous roads in Southeast
Asia is Highway 1. It links
Hanoi with Ho Chi Minh City,
although its full length runs
from Lang Son, near the
Chinese border in the north, to
Tay Ninh, near the border
with Cambodia in the south.
In all it covers a distance of
some 2000km (1250 miles). In
recent years this main artery
has been improved with the
exception of certain stretches,
mostly in the south, where it is
little better than a two-lane
rural road.

VIRGIN CAVE

One of the grottoes in Ha Long
Bay is named Virgin Cave and,
like many famous sites in
Vietnam, it honours local
womanhood. An old folk tale
records how a young fishergirl
was demanded by a rich man
in payment of a debt owed to
him by her parents. She refused
to submit to the man and was
imprisoned in the cave where
she died of starvation.

located at nearby Tam Coc. Geographically it is the
extension of adjacent land that did not sink beneath the
waves covered by Ha Long Bay. The delightful means of
visiting the caves – Tam Coc means 'three caves' – is by
rowboat along the Ngo Dong River in which ducks dive
and young boys fish with baskets. The caves are more like
tunnels than caves; the first measures 127m (413ft) long,
the second 70m (228ft) and the third 40m (130ft) long.
The boats float through them, the boat girls paddling
nimbly with one foot. At the end is a small lake where
invariably there is a boat-jam of floating vendors keen on
selling soft drinks and embroidery from nearby Van Lan
village to a captive clientele. Hanoi 'tourist cafés'
organise combined day trips to Hoa Lu and Tam Coc.

Phat Diem

Most visitors fly from Hanoi to Hue, taking day trips to tourist
sites north, east and south of the capital. For dedicated over-
landers, 30km (19 miles) southeast of Ninh Binh, Phat Diem
is the site of a noted 19th-century Catholic **cathedral**, an
eccentric oriental structure built in Sino-Vietnamese style.

Vinh and Kim Lien Village

Located some 291km (182 miles) south of Hanoi, Vinh is
notable only as an overnight stop on the overland journey
from Hanoi to Hue.

Kim Lien Village, some 14km (9 miles) northwest of Vinh, is famous as the birthplace of Ho Chi Minh. There are in fact two separate family compounds; the mother's home, where Ho was born, and his father's house, where he spent his early youth. There is also a small **museum** (mainly a photographic record of Ho) in this quiet, well-tended and curiously emotive spot.

Annam Gate (Ngang Pass)

Continuing south overland, lying on the 18th parallel, a small range of mountains forms the historical divide between the land of the Viets and the Kingdom of Champa. In colonial times, the mountains marked the division between the French provinces of Tonkin and Annam. Reaching up to a height of 1000m (3300ft), the mountains close in on Highway 1 and the road briefly joins the coast.

17th Parallel

A little way south of the town of Dong Hoi, lies the 17th Parallel that once divided North and South Vietnam. The border is physically marked by Hien Luong Bridge, carrying Highway 1 over the Ben Hai River. Prior to 1967, the northern half of the bridge was painted red and the southern half yellow. Dong Ha, the capital of Quang Tri Province, is some 72km (45 miles) north of Hue.

THE DMZ

The Demilitarized Zone (DMZ) was established during the Vietnam War as a buffer zone. It extended 5km (3 miles) on either side of the border that separated North from South Vietnam. On the southern side of the DMZ, west of Dong Ha, there were several US firebases, but now much of the area has been developed as rubber plantations. Although most visible signs of the war have vanished, unexploded mines and artillery shells still present hidden dangers, which tragically continue to cause injury and death.

Left: *These northern children find natural shelter from a passing cloudburst.*

The North at a Glance

For Ha Long Bay, the best months are from **Feb–Jul**, but don't be put off between **November** and **April** when it is mild and misty, just expect occasional rain. For the mountains, the best months are from **Apr–Jun** and **Aug–Oct**. **Apr–Sep** is hot and humid, with heavy rain. The coldest months, November to April, are grey, wet, muddy and the nights bitterly cold.

To Ha Long Bay from Hanoi, there are regular **train** (3 hours) and **minibus** (4 hours) connections. To Haiphong there are less frequent train (2 hours) and minibus (2 hours) connections. There are **boats** and **ferries** linking Ha Long Bay and Cat Ba Island, plus **hydrofoil** services between Haiphong and Cat Ba. For a quick visit, **Vietnam Airlines** flies from Ho Chi Minh City and Da Nang to Haiphong, from which there are slow (2.5 hours) and fast (1 hour) boats and hydrofoils to Cat Ba Island. The mountainous north is accessible by **car with driver** or by train or bus through tours offered by Hanoi travel agencies and tourist cafés. There is a good (overnight) train service in a soft sleeper to Lao Cai, the nearest rail point to Sa Pa. Alternatively, Vietnam Airlines operates flights to Dien Bien Phu from Hanoi (1 hour).

In **Ha Long Bay** there seems to be a shortage of metered **taxis** – no *cyclos* – so wait, **walk** or hop on the back of a **motor-bike** (*xe om*). In the highlands, **cars** and **four-wheel-drive vehicles** can be rented at a daily rate from main hotels and travel agents. Getting to remote tribes involves trekking; the less energetic can encounter tribal people in local markets (reached by **car** or **bus**).

Ha Long

The standard of hotels is good here, but the best solution is to book a two- or three-day tour, through a tourist café in Hanoi. These include the bus, sometimes a night in Ha Long Bay and a boat excursion (some with a night spent on board and a night in Cat Ba).

LUXURY

Halong Plaza, 8 Ha Long Road, tel: (33) 845 810, fax: (33) 846 867, e-mail: info@halongplaza.com www.halongplaza.com Sleek hotel offering huge rooms facing the bay.
Heritage, 88 Ha Long Road, tel: (33) 846 888, fax: (33) 846 999, e-mail: sales@heritagehalong.com www.heritagehalong.com A luxury hotel overlooking the bay.
Mithrin Hotel, Hung Thang, Cai Darn, tel: (33) 841 780, fax: (33) 841 770, e-mail: info@mithrinhotelhalong.com.vn www.mithrinhotelhalong.com

A high-rise addition to Halong with spectacular views.

MID-RANGE

Royal, Ha Long Road, tel: (33) 847 209, fax: (33) 847 148, e-mail: royalsales@hn.vnn.vn These new villas offer good value, delightful accommodation overlooking the bay.
Halong Hotel 1, Ha Long Road, tel: (33) 846 320, fax: (33) 846 318. Renovated 1930s French building with sea views.

BUDGET

Halong Hotel 2, tel: (33) 846 445 fax: (33) 640 441 **Halong Hotel 3**, tel/fax: (33) 846 316 Offering newer, but less charming accommodation than Halong Hotel 1 above.

Haiphong

LUXURY

Harbour View Hotel, 4 Tran Phu Street, tel: (31) 827 827, fax: (31) 827 828, e-mail: info@harbourviewvietnam.com www.harbourviewvietnam.com Delightful neo-colonial style.

MID-RANGE

Huu Nghi Hotel, Pho Dien Bien Phu, tel: (31) 823 310, fax: (31) 823 245, e-mail: Huunghihotel@hn.vnn.vn Central with pleasant rooms.

BUDGET

Blue Star Hotel, 34B Da Nang, tel: (31) 852 038, fax: (31) 826 414. Large hotel in a very quiet neighbourhood.

The North at a Glance

Cat Ba Island

The two best hotels are a few steps up from the waterfront. Cat Ba Town is developing so fast (electricity only arrived in 1997); doubtless there will be newer hotels by the time you arrive. Hotels become full and prices soar in Vietnamese high season (Jun–Aug). Book ahead of time or phone Mr Nguyen Van Dau (see Bamboo Forest Restaurant).

MID-RANGE

Prince Hotel, Nui Ngoc Road, tel: (31) 888 892, fax: (31) 888 899, e-mail: princeshotel@hn.vnn.vn Half a block from the sea.
Sunflower, Nui Ngoc Road, (across the street from Prince Hotel), tel: (31) 888 429, fax: (31) 888 451, e-mail: sunflower hotel@hn.vnn.vn or sales@ sunfloweronehotel.com.vn www.sunfloweronehotel.com .vn Good standard, but an eight-floor climb up stairs. (there are no lifts or elevators in Cat Ba.)

BUDGET

Strung out along Khu Cang Moi Road, overlooking the fishing port in Cat Ba Town, is a strip of budget hotels, offering the best vantage points from which to watch the fisher folk from the balconies.
Nam Duong Hotel, Khu Cang Moi, overlooking the fishing port, tel: (31) 888 586, fax: (31) 888 818. Good and

clean budget priced rooms.
Quang Duc Family Hotel, Khu Cang Moi, tel: (031) 888 231, fax: (031) 888 423. Another good choice situated on the waterfront.
Giang Son Hotel, Khu Cang Moi, tel: (31) 888 214, fax: (31) 888 379. (See Bamboo Forest Restaurant below.) One of the many overlooking the numerous fishing boats.

WHERE TO EAT

Ha Long Bay

Several restaurants along the waterfront in Ha Long Bay serve tasty seafood dishes. Look for a crowd of locals and expats.

Cat Ba Island
Bamboo Forest Restaurant, Khu Cang Moi, tel: (31) 888 654, fax: (31) 888 379, e-mail: truclamrestaurant@yahoo.com Good food overlooking the fishing port and in busy summer months the owner, Mr Nguyen Van Dau, promises to help you find a room.
Hai Long Restaurant, Khu Cang Moi, tel: (31) 861 740. Huge choice of reasonably priced Vietnamese food overlooking the bay.

TOURS AND EXCURSIONS

Numerous Hanoi travel agents organize tours to sights around Hanoi, to Ha Long Bay and the highlands:

The Highlands

To eliminate the hassle of independent touring, it is highly recommended that you book a tour through a Hanoi travel agent or tourist café. These include transport, hotels and knowledgable guides, essential for trekking.

LUXURY TOURS
Victoria Sapa Hotel, tel: (20) 871 522, fax: (20) 871 539, e-mail: resa.sapa@ victoriahotels-asia.com www.victoriahotels-asia.com Arranges a train and hotel package in private rail carriages to Sa Pa.
Bamboo Sapa Hotel, Cau May Street, Sapa, tel: (20) 871 075, fax: (20) 871 945, email: info@bamboosapaho-tel.com www.bamboosapa hotel.com Offers jeep tours to tribal markets.

See the Hanoi chapter (page 47) for both the mid-range and budget travel agents.

THE NORTH	J	F	M	A	M	J	J	A	S	O	N	D
AVERAGE TEMP. °F	61	61	66	74	81	82	84	82	81	77	70	64
AVERAGE TEMP. °C	16	16	19	23	27	28	29	28	27	25	21	18
HOURS OF SUN DAILY	3	2	1	3	6	5	7	5	6	6	5	4
RAINFALL in	1	1	2	3	9	11	15	18	12	5	1	1
RAINFALL mm	21	28	43	78	225	291	372	459	315	127	38	19
DAYS OF RAINFALL	6	9	12	10	12	14	16	17	14	8	5	5

4
Central Vietnam: Hue to Da Nang

The slender waist of **Central Vietnam** separates the flood plains of the Red River in the north from the rice bowl of the Mekong Delta to the south. The region is not only physically different due to its rugged **Truong Son Mountains** brooding over the coastal strip, it also has a distinct history, both ancient and modern.

From the 2nd to the 15th centuries AD, the region was dominated by the **Chams**, whose kingdom experienced mixed fortunes in struggles, first against the Khmer to the west, and later against the Vietnamese, who exerted pressure from the north.

Gradually wrested from the Chams by the Vietnamese, relentlessly pushing their borders south, Central Vietnam reached the peak of political importance in the early 19th century when **Hue**, the region's major city, became the capital during the **Nguyen dynasty**. Yet even when first-city status reverted to Hanoi under the French, and Ho Chi Minh City became a power base in the south, Hue remained aloof, as the epitome of cultural refinement, style and conservatism.

Laid out below the dense green of the Truong Son Mountains and straddling the placid **Perfume River** (Song Huong), despite suffering cruelly during three successive wars (1943–75), the city remains enchanting with its haunting **Citadel**, lavish **imperial tombs** and lovely **pagodas**, all of which impart a profound sense of Vietnam's recent imperial past.

Travelling south, Highway 1 cuts through beautiful land and seascapes, lush green paddies in a kaleidoscope of

DON'T MISS

*** Hue's Citadel: the former Imperial City, Hue.
*** Hue: pleasure gardens and temple tombs of the Nguyen emperors.
*** Museum of Cham Sculpture: a fine collection of 7th- to 15th-century carving, Da Nang.
*** Historic houses: Hoi An, an ancient port town in a time capsule.
** My Son: a vast complex of sacred Cham towers and temples.

Opposite: *Breathtaking views of sea and sky from Hai Van Pass, between Hue and Da Nang.*

greens hemmed in by mountains and seas. The road slowly climbs 1219m (4000ft) to **Hai Van Pass**, which the French called *Col des Nuages*, (Hill of the Clouds) and where, if it's clear, the view of the paddies and beaches below is spectacular. The road glides down past an idyllic lagoon and fishing village, **Lan Co** (where big plans for hotels were arrested by recession in Japan) to **Da Nang**, Vietnam's fourth largest city and major port.

Da Nang has played a major role in Vietnam's history. Situated in the heart of the ancient Cham Kingdom, it was in Da Nang where the French first disembarked, renaming it Tourane. Later, it was in Da Nang where the first US Marines clamoured ashore in 1965, the city serving as a pivotal US base during the **Vietnam War**.

A few miles south of Da Nang is **Hoi An**, Vietnam's earliest known port, used by the Chams who sailed up the Mekong River to trade with the Khmer and as far afield as China, Java, Malaysia, Thailand and India. During the Nguyen dynasty, the emperors allowed Hoi An a fair degree of autonomous power; by then the port town was occupied by Chinese and Japanese traders, who built houses, many of which still stand today. The prosperous port, as famous in its day during the 17th, 18th and 19th centuries as Macau or Malacca, dwindled in importance when the Thu Bon River silted up in the 19th century and port activity moved to Da Nang.

Central Vietnam

SOUTH CHINA SEA

Dien Mon
Cua Thuan An
Hue
Huong Phu
Royal Tombs
Phu Loc
Mui Chan May Dong
Bach Ma National Park
Hai Van Pass
Vinh Da Nang
Mui Da Nang
Da Nang
Marble Mountains
China Beach
Pagoda
Ba Na Hill Station
Cu Lao Cham
Hien
Dai Loc
Dien Ban
Hoi An
Temple
Tra Kieu
My Son
Pagoda
Thang Binh
NHA TRANG
VINH
Hau Trach
LAOS
14
0   50 km
0   25 miles
N

Tucked away in the hills south of Hoi An is **My Son**, the largest concentration of **monuments** standing as testament to the achievement of the Cham civilization.

HUE

Vietnam's last imperial capital, Hue, is an agreeably dispersed small city of 300,000 people lying on the banks of the **Perfume River** about 16km (10 miles) from the coast. The river divides the town. On the north bank stand the walls and moats of the Citadel, which formerly enclosed the palaces, temples and gardens of the **Imperial City** and, within that, the innermost **Forbidden Purple City**. South of the river, the old French colonial quarter developed, graced by its now restored villas and tree-shaded streets. Also lining the south bank are the major hotels as well as a few streets inland which are restaurants and banks.

When Emperor Bao Dai abdicated in 1945 with the words, 'I would rather be the citizen of an independent country than an emperor of one that is dominated', power shifted from Hue to Hanoi and Ho Chi Minh City. For all its imperial trappings, Hue found itself relegated to the role of a small provincial capital, a country cousin caught between two aggressive power blocks, the north and south. Accustomed to conservative court life laid down by tradition, Hue held to the old ways, surviving as best she could through the first rigors of **Japanese** occupation, followed by the **French Indo-China War** and then the **American War** in rapid succession.

But the old ways do have a long heritage. It is believed that the area around Hue has been occupied for at least 2000 years. Beginning as a Han Chinese military base in the 2nd century BC, the location developed as the centre of a small principality and then as one of the capitals of the Cham Kingdom. In the early 14th century, the region first became allied to the Vietnamese through

Above: *Beyond Hue and the imperial tombs, the Perfume River flows through pastoral scenery.*

RIVER EXCURSIONS

One of the most delightful ways to visit the imperial tombs is by **boat**. The city's character is largely defined by the **Perfume River** with several **major monuments**, such as Thien Mu Pagoda, being located on the river banks. Near the mouth of the river, about 12km (7.5 miles) from the city, are lagoons and Thuan An Beach, unfortunately polluted by a nearby village. Boats can be hired through tourist cafés or near the Huong Giang Hotel.

CHAM ALLIANCE

The region around Hue first became a part of Vietnam through a marriage alliance. In the late 13th century, the King of Champa, **Che Man**, offered two prefectures of his kingdom, **O** and **Ly**, in exchange for the hand of Viet Princess **Huyen Tran**. This laid the basis for the subsequent creation of the **Thuan Hoa** region. The romantic story might have had a sad ending when Che Man died a year after the marriage, because without the timely intervention of the Viet king, Huyen Tran would have perished on her husband's funeral pyre.

TET OFFENSIVE

On 31 January 1968, North Vietnamese forces attacked and occupied parts of Hue, including the Citadel. For the following 26 days, one of the bloodiest conflicts of the Vietnam War raged throughout the city as US and South Vietnamese forces fought bitterly to oust the invaders. Before their defeat, the Communists executed nearly 3000 civilians as 'uncooperative elements'. By US count, 142 Americans, 384 South Vietnamese and 5113 Communist troops died in the fighting, while most of Hue's imperial heritage was destroyed by rockets, bombs and artillery.

marriage, but was not fully annexed until the late 15th century. What was called **Phu Xuan**, in the 16th century, subsequently became the power centre of the Nguyen Lords, who held sway over the southern region of Vietnam for more than 200 years. Following the Tay Son rebellion, the first Nguyen emperor, Gia Long, chose the city as the **capital** of a newly unified Vietnam and in 1802, renamed it Hue.

A total of 13 successive Nguyen emperors were to rule from Hue (as titular rulers only during the French period) until the end of the dynasty in 1945. In the process they created, what is arguably, the loveliest city in the country.

Although violent episodes disrupted Hue's past, it is the pastoral harmony to which the city has always aspired that ultimately impresses the visitor. The city gains much from its lovely riverside location and you can sense a kind of serenity – a quiet, gentle, easy-going way that was once associated with old Asia, but now almost lost in the modern world.

Hue's Citadel ***

The heart of old Hue is the **Citadel**, the **Imperial City** of the **Nguyen** emperors, a city-within-a-city comprising three enclosures: the **Outer Fortification** (Kinh Thanh), the **Imperial Enclosure** (Hoang Thanh), where official functions took place, and the **Forbidden Purple City** (Tu Cam Thanh), the symbolic heart of the kingdom and the exclusive world of the immediate imperial family. Regrettably, the innermost complex was occupied by North Vietnamese troops during the 1968 Tet Offensive and in the fierce fighting to retake it, most of it was destroyed. Today, the site of the Forbidden Purple City is a huge, grassy expanse, where only the stone foundations of certain palaces can be traced. However, the few buildings that have survived or been restored within the Imperial Enclosure are sufficient to give an inkling of the Citadel's original grandeur, if not of its full former glory.

Construction of the Citadel was begun in 1804 by **Emperor Gia Long** and completed in the third decade of the century. Following a French design and mixing Oriental and Occidental **architecture**, it was the largest fortified complex ever built during the Vietnamese monarchy, nearly 10km (6 miles) in circumference and with walls 6m (20ft) high and 20m (66ft) thick, protected by a moat 23m (77ft) wide and 4m (13ft) deep. There were 10 entrances to the Citadel, each with a two-storey watchtower.

The Flag Tower (Ky Dai)

This is a substantial **monument** that served a defensive purpose, protecting the Citadel's main entrance. First erected in 1807 by **Gia Long** and later improved by his son, **Emperor Minh Mang**, it consists of three superimposed flat-topped pyramids, rising to a height of just over 17m (57ft). At the top stands a flagpole, twice increased in height, lastly to its present

Below: *Many of the 10 gates that pierce the Citadel walls have been severely damaged, but the eastern entrance still retains a colourful grandeur.*

37m (121ft) in 1949, making it the tallest in Vietnam. Flanking the tower are the Nine Holy Cannons (four to the east and five to the west), symbols of the **Nguyen lords** – the city's guardian spirits. Cast on the orders of Gia Long and made from brass captured from the Tay Son rebels, the cannons are purely ceremonial and represent the four seasons and the five traditional elements: fire, earth, water, metal and wood.

Ngo Mon Gate (Noon or South Gate)

The main entrance to the **Imperial City** or Great Enclosure (open daily 06:30–17:30) is directly behind the Flag Tower. **Ngo Mon Gate** is one of four original gateways, the others being: the Gate of Peace (Hoa Binh) in the north, the Gate of Humanity (Hien Nhon) in the east, and the Gate of Virtue (Chuong Duc) in the west. All are monumental and ornate affairs, although Ngo Mon Gate is the largest with five doors (the others have three), the central one used exclusively by the **emperor**.

The gate is surmounted by the **Ngu Phun Pavilion** (the Pavilion of Five Phoenixes), flanked by twin belvederes. From this vantage point the emperor presided over important ceremonial occasions. The centre of the structure, where the emperor would appear, is roofed with yellow tiles, and there are green tiles on either side.

Below: *Only royal princes were allowed to stand within the walls of the Palace of Supreme Harmony, where the emperor would receive foreigh emissaries during ceremonial occassions.*

Palace of Supreme Harmony (Dien Thai Hoa)

Beyond Ngo Mon Gate, a bridge (formerly, only for the emperor's use) crosses a lotus pond to the **Great Rites Court** (San Dai Trieu), where court mandarins stood in attendance in order of rank. Facing this is the Palace of Supreme Harmony, the Imperial City's principal building, where court ceremonies were held and the emperor gave audiences. Measuring 44m (144ft) long and just over 30m (100ft) wide, this wooden palace was built in 1805. The interior is notable for its 80 huge red lacquered ironwood columns, carved and painted with gilt dragon and cloud designs, symbolizing the meeting of the monarch and his subjects.

Halls of the Mandarins

Facing the courtyard behind the **Palace of Supreme Harmony** are two buildings (restorations) where the mandarins used to prepare for court ceremonies (in the building on the left, visitors can pose for photographs sitting on a throne wearing royal robes). In the courtyard two 17th-century cauldrons commemorate victories of the **Nguyen Lords** over the Trinh.

The Forbidden Purple City (Tu Cam Thanh)

Once the Great Golden Gate, the most magnificent of all the Imperial City's gates, led from behind the Palace of Supreme Harmony into the inner sanctum of the Forbidden Purple City. Sadly, this gate was lost during anti-French struggles in 1947; the rest was destroyed in the **Tet Offensive** of 1968. The first building to have been restored is a small but elaborately decorated two-storey **library** (Thai Binh Lau) pavilion halfway down the east side of the compound.

Royal Theatre

The most stunning, newly rebuilt building stands off to the right from the courtyard behind the Palace of Supreme Harmony (then turn left). This dazzling new theatre is built to the original plans with thick red lacquered pillars embellished with gilt clouds and dragons. It gives one the impression of just having stepped into the glorious imperial past. Performances of traditional music and Vietnamese opera (*tuong*) are being planned.

Back at the Palace of Supreme Harmony, following a leafy lane off to the left are several more impressive temples. Through a pretty, newly restored gate (on the left) you can see three temples standing side by side.

DYNASTY URNS

The nine dynastic urns in front of The To Mieu were cast during the reign of Minh Mang. Hundreds of craftsmen from all over the country were involved in their production. Decorated with suns, moons, dragons, mountains, natural landscapes and historic events to represent the everlasting power of the empire, the urns are estimated to weigh between 1900kg (4189lb) and 2500kg (5521lb) each.

TINH TAM LAKE

Located a short distance north of the Imperial City is Ho Tinh Tam, Lake of the Serene Heart, once a beauty spot of ancient Hue. The site is a vestige of a tributary of the Perfume River, which was diked here and broadened by Emperor Gia Long to make a rectangular lake 1.42km (0.8 miles) in circumference. Two small islands in the middle of the lake were originally occupied by storehouses for gunpowder, but Emperor Minh Mang had these removed and replaced by palaces and pavilions to become an imperial pleasure ground. Minh Mang is said to have composed 10 poems inspired by 10 views of the lake.

Hung To Mieu

The temple was built in 1804 to honour the parents of the first Nguyen emperor, Gia Long. His father, **Nguyen Phuc Luan**, had been killed in battle against the Trinhs of the north. Restored in 1997, it glistens with red lacquer. A few framed photographs are revealing as to how **feudalism** existed in Vietnam in the recent past. Duy Tan, 11th to reign, stares fixedly back from a black and white photograph. Anti-French, both he and his father, Than Thai, were exiled by the French to Reunion.

The To Mieu

First built in 1821, this building holds the funerary tablets and shrines dedicated to the first ten emperors of the Nguyen dynasty, the three serving under the French (Ham Nghi, Thanh Thai and Duy Tan), only having been added in 1959.

Nine Dynastic Urns

These ornate bronze vessels are placed in the shade of the Hien Lam Pavilion, in front of the Mieu Temple. They were cast in 1822 to symbolize the sovereignty of the dynasty and are dedicated to (the first) nine Nguyen rulers. The central and most elaborate urn is that of Gia Long, dynasty founder, who ordered them cast.

Hien Lam Pavilion

Recently rebuilt and restored, this is an elegant three-storey memorial temple dedicated, once again, to the Nguyen emperors. Pure poetry in architecture.

Minh Duong

Returning along the leafy lane, turn to the left for another complex under restoration.

This surprisingly unroyal 19th-century, French-style **villa** (Minh Duong) – with a wrap-around porch (not open) – first served the queen mother and first wife of Emperor Dong Khan, **Empress Thanh Cung**, as a private clinic. Later it became the residence of the last emperor, Bao Dai. Beyond are two courtyards surrounded by temples under restoration.

BEYOND HUE'S CITADEL

Lively **Dong Ba Market**, on Tran Hung Dao Street, is on the north bank of the river next to the bus station. It is best to visit early in the morning when the fish come in.

Dieu De National Pagoda

Located at 102 Bach Dang Street, directly east of the Citadel, is a pagoda distinguished by its four towers. It was formerly under the direct patronage of the emperor, hence 'national'. In the 60s, it was a hotbed of Buddhist opposition to the war and the South Vietnamese government and it was raided by the police in 1966.

Chua Ong Pagoda

A little way to the north, this large Chinese Buddhist pagoda dates from the 19th century. It has a somewhat interesting interior, although the building was badly damaged during the **Tet Offensive**.

Tin Lanh

The only church on the north bank of the river, stands a short distance northeast of Dieu De National Pagoda.

Quang Pagoda

On Nguyen Chi Thanh Street, is Hue's largest Theravada Buddhist temple. Although the building is modern, its Sri Lankan-influenced architecture sets it apart from the horizontal style of Mahayana Buddhist pagodas.

Thien Mu Pagoda
(Pagoda of the Heavenly Lady) ★★★

Standing in splendid isolation on a hillock overlooking the Perfume River some 4km (2.5 miles) upstream from the Citadel, this is one of Vietnam's most famous sights.

Above: *The nine dynastic urns commemorating the first nine Nguyen emperors stand beside Hien Lam Pavilion in the Citadel in Hue.*

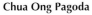

NGUYEN DYNASTY

Gia Long: 1802–19
Minh Mang: 1820–40
Thieu Tri: 1840–47
Tu Duc: 1848–83
Duc Duc: 1883 (dethroned after three days)
Hiep Hoa: 1883 (assassinated)
Kien Phuc: 1883–84
Ham Nghi: 1884–85 (dethroned)
Dong Khan: 1885–89
Than Thai: 1889–1907 (deposed)
Duy Tan: 1907–16 (deposed)
Khai Dinh: 1916–25
Bao Dai: 1925–45 (abdicated)

Legend has it that the pagoda was founded in 1601 after an old woman dressed in a red gown and green trousers appeared on the hill and prophesied: 'Soon a true king will come here and build a pagoda that will attract and converge all the heavenly forces and energies of the Dragon Veins.' After having uttered these words the woman vanished. Accepting the prophesy as his destiny, Lord Nguyen Hoang, the first of ten Nguyen feudal lords to rule over the area during the 17th and 18th centuries, built a pagoda, which he named 'Heavenly Lady'. None of his original buildings survive; those seen today date from works carried out in 1714–15 and 1844–46.

Dominating the entire compound is the wedding-cake architecture of the seven-storey Phuoc Duyen Tower, 21m (69ft) high, built by Emperor Thieu Tri in 1844. Each storey represents an incarnation of the Buddha. Beside the tower is the main sanctuary dominated by an enormous **laughing Buddha**. The sanctuary also contains a stele carved in 1715, set on the back of a marble tortoise. A pavilion on the left houses a huge bell cast in 1710, weighing over two tons. Nearby are shrines to Quan Vo (God of War) and Quan An (Goddess of Mercy). The site commands splendid views out over the Perfume River, especially when the flamboyant trees are blooming. Services are at dawn and 16:00. It is also a good place to buy **paintings** on silk.

FIERY PROTEST

On 11 June 1963, Thich Quang Duc, a 73-year-old monk from Thien Mu Pagoda, immolated himself in Ho Chi Minh City to protest at the Ngo Dinh Diem government's persecution of Buddhists. The event, making world headlines in a famous press photograph, set an example for the self-immolation of other monks and nuns, and accelerated the downfall of Diem, who was killed in a military coup on 2 November. The Austin car in which Thich Quang Duc drove to Ho Chi Minh City is preserved in a building behind Thien Mu Pagoda's main sanctuary.

SOUTH OF HUE'S RIVER

The area once known as the 'New City', the French quarter, with its wide boulevards, spacious villas, new hotels, restaurants and government buildings, feels quite modern by comparison.

Bao Quoc Pagoda

A pagoda has existed on this site off Dien Bien Phu Street since 1670, although there have been numerous renovations. Several buildings occupy the garden-like complex where there are also monks' tombs.

Tu Dam Pagoda

On Dien Bien Phu Street, a short distance south of Bao Quoc, Tu Dam pagoda derives its reputation from a tradition of militant Buddhism. The pagoda was the centre of a reformed school of **Buddhism**, originating in China in the 1920s, and it was here that the Unified Vietnamese Buddhist Association was formed in the 1950s. During the following decade, the pagoda was a centre of opposition to President Diem and the war. In 1968, it was a target of the North Vietnamese forces during their Tet Offensive.

Phu Cam Cathedral

East of Tu Dam Pagoda is the headquarters of the **Hue diocese**. A church has existed on the site since the 17th century. Construction of the present building begun in 1963, although it was left unfinished when work was halted in 1975.

Notre Dame Cathedral

Hue's other cathedral on Nguyen Hue Street is well worth seeking out for its curious architecture, which mixes monumental European and Oriental styles – notice the three-tiered pagoda-like spire. Although dating from the mid-20th century, the building is wonderfully self-assured.

HUE'S IMPERIAL TOMBS ★★★

The royal tombs – think of pleasure grounds and temples rather than cemeteries and mausoleums – of the Nguyen emperors who ruled in Hue from 1802 to 1945, are located south of the city amidst picturesque wooded hills on both sides of the Perfume River. Combining park-like landscapes and lakes with certain traditional

---

HUE MUSEUMS

The Imperial Museum is located at 3 Le Truc Street. Despite the loss of many royal treasures during colonial and war years, the remaining exhibits bequeathed by the imperial family are fascinating and include ceremonial robes, furniture, ceramics and other objets d'art from the palace. Originally part of the Citadel, the building itself is an architectural museum piece. **Ho Chi Minh Museum**, 9 Le Loi Street, houses a small collection of photographs, documents and personal belongings.

Opposite: *The seven-storey tower of Thien Mu Pagoda measures 21m (69ft), each storey containing an altar to a different Buddha.*
Below: *The graceful interior of Hue's Catholic Cathedral.*

HO CHI MINH TRAIL

A major factor in the North's war effort and a symbol of the Communists' determination, the Ho Chi Minh Trail was not a single path but rather a 15,000km (9300 miles) network of secret and camouflaged tracks. Along this vital conduit, the North Vietnamese shipped arms and equipment to their guerrilla comrades in the South, initially by bicycle and later by truck. A section of the trail runs through the west of Da Nang from where excursions can be arranged – check with hotel or local tour agencies.

architectural elements, each tomb is an extensive affair comprising this sequence: a pavilion housing a stele recording the emperor's achievements; a brick-paved court of honour where life-sized stone mandarins and animal figures stand in attendance; a temple of the soul enshrining the funerary tablet and precious objects belonging to the emperor; a mausoleum and additional houses for guards, servants and retainers. Although they follow a general traditional pattern, most of the tombs were designed and built during their future occupants' lifetimes and so display variations that reflect their different characters and personalities.

The tombs are spread out over a wide area and can be visited by boat or bus tour, by taxi, motorbike or bike. Included on the tours are:

The Tomb of Khai Dinh

Located about 10km (6 miles) south of Hue, this tomb is hardly the most representative, but must be seen for comparison. The Vietnamese don't like it very much. It eschews all efforts at Oriental restraint and makes a delirious bid for immortality through a huge, garish baroque creation. Emperor Khai Dinh ruled from 1916 to 1925 and his tomb was built between 1920 and 1931, much influenced by his notion of European grandeur. The approach is up three steep flights of dragon-flanked steps, which open onto an expanse of statue-studded courtyard. The *pièce de résistance* is the interior of the mausoleum, a claustrophobic extravaganza of porcelain and glass mosaic and the tomb itself is topped by a larger-than-life gilt statue of Khai Dinh himself. A masterpiece of kitch on a grand scale.

Below: *Stone mandarins stand in permanent attendance in the court of honour at Khai Dinh's tomb.*

The Tomb of Minh Mang

About 12km (7.5 miles) from Hue, Minh Mang's tomb is on the opposite river bank (a boat can be hired for the short crossing). Minh Mang, possibly the greatest of the Nguyen emperors, ruled from 1820 to 1840 and his tomb was completed in 1843. His burial site comprises classical architectural forms, methodically and harmoniously laid out in a satisfyingly tranquil landscaped setting of lotus ponds, flowering trees and lakes. Combining solemnity with symmetry, the tomb is set within an oval-walled enclosure. Along the east-west axis, running 700m (765yd) from the main gate, are the principal features: the court of honour, the

stele pavilion, Hien Duc Gate, Sung An Temple, Hoang Trach Gate, Trung Dao Bridge, Minh Law Pavilion (atop a three-tiered terrace) and, beyond a crescent-shaped lake, the circular walled burial mound.

Above: *Minh Mang's tomb blends the beauty of its natural setting with majestic architecture and exquisite stone sculpture.*

The Tomb of Tu Duc

Tu Duc ruled from 1848 to 1883 – the Nguyen dynasty's longest reign. The tomb, located about 8km (5 miles) from Hue on the south bank, was built between 1864 and 1867 in what was then tiger infested jungle. It was designed by the emperor as a secluded poetic fairyland where he could write poetry and enjoy life's pleasures and, in death, find a harmonious resting place. Comprising some 50 structures enclosed by a 1500m (1640yd) wall, the tomb is entered via the Vu Khiem Gate in the south. To the right is the delightful Luu Khiem Lake, with Tinh Khiem islet in the middle. Straight ahead is the Du Khiem Pavilion and, across the lake, Xung Khiem Pavilion – built over the water on stilts – where Tu Duc used to sit and compose poetry. West of Du Khiem Pavilion is the Hoa Khiem Temple (used as a palace during Tu Duc's lifetime), and a complex of buildings, including, on the right, Minh Khiem royal theatre.

HILL STATION

A cool retreat from Hue is offered by Mt Bach Ma, an old French hill station, now a national park, located 55km (34 miles) southwest of the city. Situated at an altitude of more than 1400m (4590ft), Bach Ma is reported to hold 125 species of wildlife, including more than 800 species of birds. Bach Ma offers walking trails and fine views amid lush greenery and a year-round spring-like climate. Facilities are few and at present you must hire a guide. Best from February to September.

Da Nang

Vinh Da Nang

THANH BINH GUESTHOUSE

Thanh Binh Beach

Thach Thang Lagoon

SAIGON TOURANE (H)(H) DA NANG

THU BON (H)

Ly Thuong Kiet
ELEGANT (H)

Nguyen Du

Ly Tu Trong
(H) HAI VAN

ROYAL (H)(H) BACH DANG
AMI

Quang Trung

Cao Dai Temple
Haiphong Church
Da Nang Railway Station

BINH DUONG (H)

Le Duan

RIVERSIDE

Phan Dinh Phung   Ferry Terminal

CHINA BEACH

SONG HAN

Tran Cao Van

Le Duan

Stadium

Hung Vuong

Con Market

THANH (H)
THANH

Han Market

Ly Thai To

PACIFIC (H)(H)
Nguyen Trai

Pri Lu 2   Da Nang Cathedral
Tran Quoc Toan (H) DAESCO
Kim Do
Le Hong Phong   PHUONG DONG

Hoang Van Thu

Le Dinh Duong

Song Han

Phap Lam Pagoda

Tam Bao Pagoda

Museum of Cham Sculpture

Pho Da Pagoda

MARBLE MOUNTAINS, FURAMA RESORT DANANG

0   500 m
0   150 yd

N

The court of honour, stele pavilion and mausoleum are directly north of the Hoa Khiem Temple complex, although the emperor's mortal remains are not here; the site of his burial is unknown. Fine landscaping and an atmosphere of oriental fantasy distinguish the site.

DA NANG

An exceptional natural setting has given Da Nang its historic importance, while its relative distance from political power centres has assured a certain individuality. Da Nang is Vietnam's fourth-largest city with a population of 764,500 and it lies 754km (471 miles) south of Hanoi and 944km (580 miles) north of Ho Chi Minh City. Hue is only about 100km (62 miles) to the north, separated by the Hai Van Pass, a natural divide, geographically and meteorologically.

The port city sits on the west bank of the mouth of the Han River, which flows out into a horseshoe bay. Protected from the South China Sea by a spur of land on the west and a broadly curving coastline to the east, the bay is a huge and perfect natural harbour.

Hoi An (see page 78) was originally the region's principal **port** and centre of foreign trade. Da Nang first became known in the 17th and 18th centuries as the gateway – and later a battleground – for the first European arrivals, the Spanish, followed by the French. Rechristened Tourane by the French, Da Nang became a French trade concession area in 1787.

In the 19th century Da Nang succeeded Hoi An as Central Vietnam's major port. In 1847, it entered another phase of history when a French man-of-war sailed into the harbour, thereby sparking the struggle for colonial acquisition. The original intention had been to land at Hue, but the river estuary was too shallow for the French ships.

Major development of Da Nang began after the partition of the country in 1954. A decade later the place became famous as the spot where the first US combat troops to arrive in Vietnam landed on 8 March 1965. The port was subsequently transformed into a huge American naval and air base (with the longest jet aircraft runway in Southeast Asia). As such an important **military target**, Da Nang drew so much enemy fire that it became known as 'Rocket City'.

Today, Da Nang remains an important port for both the agricultural products of Central Vietnam and potential exports from southern Laos. The city exudes an air of free-wheeling entrepreneurism and has already enjoyed comparatively rapid economic development.

Museum of Cham Sculpture (Bao Tang Cham) ***

Da Nang's one not-to-be-missed sight is the Museum of Cham Sculpture, located in the southern part of the city at the corner of Tran Phu and Le Dinh Duong Streets. Da Nang lies at the centre of the area once dominated by the Chams and the museum houses one of the world's finest collections of Cham sculpture, (visit also the Guimet Museum in Paris and the History Museum in Ho Chi Minh City). Open daily from 07:30 to 11:00 and 13:30 to 16:30.

Marvellously accomplished sandstone carvings of gods, goddesses, beasts and celestial dancing girls are a glorious testament to the great artistic talents of the Chams.

Opened in 1916 under the patronage of the very highly respected Ecole Française d'Extrème Orient and enlarged in 1936, the

CHAM ARCHITECTURE

Brick was the prime medium of Cham architecture. Of excellent quality, the bricks were rubbed smooth and finely bonded with a mortar made from vegetable matter. Temples consist essentially of a tall, square sanctuary tower, a square entrance hall and a steep roof of several storeys in descending size. Pilasters and projections give the towers their characteristic graceful proportions. Smaller attendant buildings included libraries usually with corbelled brick roofs and halls.

Below: *Da Nang's airy Museum of Cham Sculpture has some fine exhibits, dating from the 7th to the 15th century.*

museum has approximately 300 exhibits dating from the 7th to the 15th centuries. According to legend, the Chams sprang from **Uroja** – the mother goddess. She was one of a trinity of deities although she was the only goddess. She is also confusingly known as Po Nagar. In the Cham language her name translates as 'woman's breast', which explains the abundance of rounded breasts used as borders around friezes and pedestals. Much influenced by **Hinduism** and later **Buddhism**, the Chams adopted **Sanskrit** as a religious language. Their own language originated from Malayo-Polynesian roots and to this day the Chams around Phan Rang, further south, speak a language related to one spoken by a tribe in Borneo. A worthwhile booklet on sale at the museum is written by former director Tran Ky Phuong and it provides a good general introduction to Cham art.

Other City Sights

The following attractions can easily be covered on a walking tour heading west, and then heading north from the Museum.

Tam Bao Pagoda, at 253 Phan Chu Trinh Street, is a Theravada Buddhist pagoda, the only one in Da Nang, distinguished by a five-tiered tower and 'begging monks', who wear brown robes. Inside on the right is an emaciated begging Buddha, on the left a seated Buddha.

Pho Da Pagoda, at 340 Phan Chu Trinh Street, is a pretty yellow pagoda with a graceful three-tiered yellow and green tiled roof. A large 'gold' statue of Buddha dominates the interior. This particular incarnation, **Thich Ca Mu Ni**, sits amongst statues of bodhisattvas, those who have attained Nirvana, but chose to remain in this world to help others along the way.

BEST BEACHES

China Beach is Da Nang's best beach, situated about 14km (8.5 miles) south of the city. This 20km (12 miles) sandy beach was used for rest and recreation during the Vietnam War and it was made famous by a US TV series of the same name. **Lang Co** is an idyllic spot with all the right ingredients – an unspoilt fishing village,a blue lagoon and a sandy beach – and it is located about 40km (25 miles) north of Da Nang. **Nam O Beach** lies about 15km (9 miles) north of Da Nang. **Thanh Binh Beach** is the closest to Da Nang at 2km (1.5 miles), but it is usually crowded and therefore not recommended. **My Khe Beach**, about 6km (4 miles) from central Da Nang, is a better beach but an undertow makes swimming unsafe.

Phap Lam Pagoda, at 574 Ong Ich Khiem Street, looks quite old with its mossy tiled roof, but it was built in 1934. A serene statue of Quan Am, Goddess of Mercy, presides over the garden and seated in her own tiny pavilion is the figure of a highly colourful, multi-armed goddess, Thien Nhon.

Da Nang Cathedral, on Tran Phu Street, about four blocks north of the Cham Museum, was built in 1923. It is a delightful pink and white Gothic confection that looks like something turned out by Wedgewood.

Cao Dai Temple, on Haiphong Street, is the second largest Cao Dai Temple in Vietnam (after Tay Ninh). From the huge altarpiece globe, the characteristic 'divine eye', the religion's symbol, stares out at the worshippers. A sign translates as 'All religions have the same reason'.

AROUND DA NANG
Marble Mountains (Ngu Hanh Son)

About 12km (7.5 miles) south of Da Nang, five extraordinary hills rise from the coastal plain. They are actually limestone with marble outcrops and each is dedicated to one of the five traditional elements: water (*thuy son*), fire (*hoa son*), earth (*tho son*), metal or gold (*kim son*) and wood (*moc son*). The spot has been sacred since the time of the Chams when grottoes in the hills were turned into first Hindu and, then later, Buddhist shrines.

The hill most visited is Thuy Son. You need to be a bit of a mountain goat to negotiate the steps, although children are always on hand to act as guides.

Atmospheric with their looming statuary shrouded in incense smoke, the main sights on Thuy Son are Linh Ung Pagoda, **Tam Thai Pagoda** (built by Emperor Minh Mang in 1825) and the spectacularly cavernous **Huyen Khong Cave**, a site of Buddhist pilgrimage. Hoa Hai village at the foot of the mountains specializes in carved marble statues and inexpensive souvenirs. Many prefer to watch the craftsmen at work rather than climb the mountain.

COOL ESCAPE

Located about 45km (28 miles) west of Da Nang is **Ba Na**, once a hill retreat where French colonials escaped the summer heat. The scenery and views are magnificent, while the 1460m (4790ft) altitude ensures cool temperatures. The new Ba Na Resort, tel (511) 818 044, offers simple, inexpensive rooms and there is also a restaurant.

Opposite: *An uninterrupted stretch of sand and sea, China Beach, at the foot of the Marble Mountains, was once a 'Rest and Relaxation' spot for US military personnel during the Vietnam War.*
Below: *One of the five Marble Mountains contained a field hospital that was bombed, leaving a hole open to the sky.*

HOI AN AND AROUND

Hoi An has an embarrassment
of small café's and restaurants,
which makes it a good spot for
lingering. A delightful excursion can be taken from Hoi An
to nearby Cau Dai Beach, an
easy bike or mototaxi ride
some 5km (3 miles) east of
town down Tran Hung Dao
Street. The beach has fine
white sand and the water is
clear and good for bathing.

Below: *An important 16th-
century trading port on the
route between China and
India, Hoi An is now a
tranquil town on the banks
of the Thu Bon River.*

Hoi An

Situated on the banks of the Thu Bon River 30km (19
miles) south of Da Nang, the little town of Hoi An (known
to the Chinese as Faifo) feels caught in a time warp. It is
filled with the atmosphere of centuries past. This one-time
international trading port, now a quaint backwater, has an
impressive heritage.

Archaeologists believe the site to have been inhabited
for at least 2000 years, while its history as a seaport reaches
back to the 2nd century AD, when it was the principal port
for Champa. A fresh lease of life arrived in the 16th century
when a wave of Chinese and Japanese settlers established
Hoi An as a port-of-call on the China–India trade route.
Then came European merchants and missionaries, first the
Portuguese, later the Dutch, Spanish, French and British,
who called in at Hoi An to purchase high-grade silk, herbal
medicines, mother-of-pearl, areca nuts, lacquer, porcelain
and other exotic cargoes.

Although badly damaged during the **Tay Son rebellion**
in the late 18th century, Hoi An had flourished as one of
Southeast Asia's most important ports until the 19th century
when the **Thu Bon River** silted up and prevented the
passage of ocean-going vessels. Hoi An's economic clock
stopped, which resulted in how much the town appears
today as it must have done a century or more ago –
preserved like a fly in amber.

Declared a **World Heritage Site** by UNESCO, the
wise local authorities have claimed the entire town
a pedestrian area – with the exception of bikes, *cyclos*
(bicycle trishaws) and motorbikes. The traditional
temples, shrines, Chinese
communal houses and a few
private houses are open to
the public with a ticket that
includes a choice of several.
To visit them all, simply buy
two, or even three tickets.
Narrow streets, huddled
wooden shophouses and a
corrugated skyline of crusty

tiled roofs smothered in morning glories exude antiquity. Furthermore, Hoi An probably offers the best, most concentrated shopping street in all of Vietnam for all manner of crafts, antiques, clothes, silk, lacquer, ceramics, bronze and wood statues, embroidery, marble and jade jewellery. Add a plethora of excellent tiny restaurants, some overlooking the river, and Hoi An appeals as an exciting place to linger.

Sightseeing in Hoi An ***

Hoi An could be visited on a day excursion from Da Nang, but staying over affords the leisure to absorb the town's atmosphere and genuine charm. The town is small and best explored on foot (or *cyclo*), with most major sights on or near **Tran Phu Street**, the main east–west artery running parallel to, and a couple of blocks back from, the waterfront. The following is a suggested walking tour starting near the market.

Quan Cong Temple and **Quan Am Pagoda** stand back to back at the corner of Nguyen Hue and Tran Phu Streets, opposite the market. Dating from the mid-17th century, these are small but atmospheric Chinese temples enclosed around a central courtyard. The former is dedicated to legendary Chinese warrior Quan Cong, whose large and colourful papier-mâché statue is flanked by those of one of his generals, **Chau Xuong**, and a mandarin, **Quan Binh**.

Situated across the street is lively **Hoi An Market**, extending down to the river and selling dry goods as well as fresh produce.

East from Quan Cong Temple are two Chinese assembly halls (where Tran Phu Street becomes Nguyen Duy Hieu Street). Hai Nam Assembly Hall was built in 1883 and it has an ornate interior. A bit further east, beyond the intersection with Hoang Dieu Street, the Trieu Chau Assembly Hall is a 200-year-old building with some exceptional woodcarving.

Retracing one's steps back west along Tran Phu Street, the **Fukien Chinese Assembly Hall** stands opposite 35 Tran Phu Street. Dating originally from the late 17th century, and rebuilt at the end of the 19th, the hall is

Above: *Chinese influence can be seen in the ornamental detail of Hoi An's domestic architecture.*

KHE SANH

In early 1968, the USA feared its base at Khe Sanh, south of the DMZ (Demilitarized Zone) near Huong Hoa, could become another Dien Bien Phu, and reinforced it accordingly. Although not defeated, Khe Sanh was besieged for 77 days in one of the bloodiest – and arguably most pointless – battles of the war. As many as 500 US Marines and 10,000–15,000 North Vietnamese were killed; 67,500 metric tons of bombs were dropped in the area, and buried explosives are still killing people at Khe Sanh today.

Above: *The graceful curve of the Japanese Covered Bridge suggests the movement of the waters beneath.*
Below: *A neatly dressed schoolteacher on her way to class in Hoi An.*

dedicated to Thien Hau, Goddess of the Sea.

The house at 77 Tran Phu Street is a fine and well-preserved example of Hoi An's domestic architecture of some 300 years ago. It is still a private house but open to visitors.

Towards the western end of Tran Phu Street, just beyond the intersection with Nhi Trung Street, is the 18th-century assembly hall dedicated to **Quang Dong**. At the end of the street is the Japanese Covered Bridge, an 18m (60ft) wooden structure built at the end of the 16th century by the Japanese community. The eastern and western ends of the bridge are flanked by statues of a pair of monkeys and a pair of dogs, placed here because construction of the bridge was begun in the Year of the Monkey and was completed in the Year of the Dog. There is a tiny pagoda hidden within the bridge.

Tan Ky House, at 101 Nguyen Thai Hoc Street, is a sumptuous traditional old house. It has been, one might say, sculpted of local hard wood, its well-preserved architecture and antique decoration offering a glimpse of how prosperous Hoi An merchants lived a century or more ago. This private house, open to visitors, has elegant inlaid mother-of-pearl columns decorated in a delightful floral design.

From Nguyen Thai Hoc Street, it is a short walk to the charming little waterfront where boats can be hired for the trip across the river to **Cam Kim Island**, long renowned for its boat builders and woodcarvers. Here, there is a project to train young people to carve in the age-old tradition. It is well worth visiting.

On the northern outskirts of town, **Chuc Thanh Pagoda** is a restored version of Hoi An's oldest temple, originally founded in 1454. Beyond Chuc Thanh stands **Phuoc Lam Pagoda**, which dates from the 17th century.

My Son **

Hidden away in a secret valley, My Son represents the most extensive Cham **ruins** in Vietnam. Thought to have been an important Cham intellectual and religious centre and probably the burial place of Cham kings, it was named a **World Heritage Site** in 2000 by UNESCO. Bearing in mind that during the Vietnam War, My Son was used as a Viet Cong field headquarters and therefore attracted heavy bombing (until a curator of the Guimet Museum in Paris sent a plea to President Nixon to stop the bombing) and the surrounding area was heavily mined, it is somewhat surprising that as much remains as there is.

Of the 68 **monuments** built at My Son, fewer than 20 remain standing. Some restoration work has been done and more is planned. It is nevertheless thought-provoking to wander amongst the red brick ruins of towers and temples, some built as early as the 8th century.

Honouring **Hindu** divinities, particularly Siva, and dedicated to Cham kings, the most characteristic structures are towers with four porticoes. The towers display fine brickwork (ingeniously, newly-built temples were surrounded by fires and baked in a kind of open kiln), along with varying degrees of stone sculpture, bas-relief carvings and other rather highly accomplished decorative work.

Set in a river valley surrounded by hills, the monuments of My Son comprise 10 main groups, which archaeologists have designated by letters and divided by numbers. Most rewarding are the two adjacent temple complexes (originally square enclosures) titled B and C. The former is the larger and although only the base of the main sanctuary remains, the smaller attendant buildings are comparatively well preserved.

My Son is located about 60km (37 miles) south of Da Nang and west of Tra Kieu. The site is no longer difficult to reach – only the last 2km (1 mile) require a jeep, provided in the price of the ticket. There are even new western toilets (and bidets!) Day tours can be arranged through Da Nang or Hoi An hotels or travel agents.

Above: *The Chams honoured Hindu divinities, as the sinuous curves of this stone carving show.*

CHAM CAPITALS

Tra Kieu was the site of Singhapura (Lion Citadel), Cham capital from the 4th to the 8th centuries, although only traces of the ramparts can be seen today. Some 20km (12 miles) from My Son, Dong Duong was the city of Indrapura, the 9th- to 10th-century Cham capital and site of an important late 9th-century Buddhist monastery.

Central Vietnam at a Glance

Dec–Mar is generally best for Central Vietnam. Hue is best from **Feb–Jun**.

Hue is served by **domestic flights** from Hanoi, Ho Chi Minh City and Da Nang. Da Nang receives **international flights** from Bangkok, Hong Kong and Singapore; domestic flights from Ho Chi Minh City, Nha Trang, Hue and Hanoi. The Hanoi–Ho Chi Minh City **railway** links Hue and Da Nang. Hoi An is reached by **taxi** or **bus** from Da Nang, 30km (18 miles).

Bicycles, *cyclos* and metered **taxis** are readily available.

Hue
LUXURY
Hotel Saigon Morin, 30 Le Loi Street, tel: (54) 823 526, fax: (54) 825 155, e-mail: sgmorin@dng.vnn.vn www.morinhotel.com.vn Elegant colonial hotel built around a pleasant courtyard; some rooms have river views.

MID-RANGE
Huong Giang Hotel, 51 Le Loi Street, tel: (54) 822 122, fax: (54) 823 102, e-mail: hghotel@dng.vnn.vn A riverfront location with a delightful Hue style bamboo, cane and lacquer decor – the lobby resembles a royal palace.
Century Riverside Inn, 49 Le

Loi Street, tel: (54) 823 390, fax: (54) 823 394, e-mail: cenhotvn@dng.vnn.vn www.centuryriversidehue.com Located next to Huong Giang.

BUDGET
l'Indochine (Dong Duong) Hotel, 2 Hung Vuong Street, tel: (54) 823 866, fax: (54) 825 910, email: indochine-hotel@dng.vnn.vn Value for money.
Thuan Hoa Hotel, 7 Nguyen Tri Phuong Street, tel: (54) 822 553, fax: (54) 822 470, e-mail: t_hoahtl@dng.vnn.vn Huge rooms, a few blocks from the bridge leading to the Citadel.

Da Nang
LUXURY
Furama Resort Da Nang, 68 Ho Xuan Huong (China Beach), tel: (511) 847 333, fax: (511) 847 666, e-mail: furama dn@hn.vnn.vn Set in tropical gardens on China Beach a few kilometres from town. Vietnam's first five-star resort.

MID-RANGE
Saigon Tourane Hotel, 5 Dong Da, Hai Chau District, tel: (511) 821 021, fax: (511) 895 285, e-mail: sgtouran@dng.vnn.vn www.saigontourane.com.vn The best in central Da Nang.

BUDGET
Elegant Hotel, 22A Bach Dang Street, tel: (511) 892 893, fax: (511) 835 179, e-mail: elegant@dng.vnn.vn Lovely rooms with a river view.

Hoi An
Everyone's favourite, pedestrianized Hoi An has sprouted three new luxury resorts a few kilometres out on the beach and numerous privately-owned mini hotels. Warning: It still gets tightly booked around Tet (*see* page 124).

LUXURY
Victoria Hoi An Resort, Cua Dai Beach, tel: (510) 927 040, fax: (510) 927 041, e-mail: resa.hoian@ victoriahotels-asia.com French EEM group's newest, very pricey establishment.
Hoi An Riverside Resort & Spa, 175 Cua Dai Road, tel: (510) 864 800, fax: (510) 864 900, e-mail: hoianriver@dng.vnn.vn A stylish hotel in lush gardens with superb views of the river, rice paddies and the sea.
Hoi An Beach Resort, 01 Cua Dai Road, tel: (510) 927 011, fax: (510) 927 019, e-mail: reservation@hoian beachresort.com.vn www. hoianbeachresort.com.vn A younger and more elegant sister of the hotel in town.

MID-RANGE
Hoi An Hotel, 10 Tran Hung Dao Street, Hoi An Town, tel: (510) 861 445, fax: (510) 861 636, e-mail: hoianhotel@dng.vnn.vn www.hoiantourist.com This old French colonial hotel has had beautiful new rooms and a snazzy pool added.

Central Vietnam at a Glance

BUDGET

Pho Hoi Riverside Resort, T1
Cam Nam Village, tel: (510)
862 628, fax: (510) 862 626,
e-mail: phohoiht@dng.vnn.vn
www.phohoiriversidehoian.
com On the river just over
the bridge. There is good
basic accommodation and a
pleasant riverside pavilion
restaurant.

WHERE TO EAT

Hue

Hue has a number of interesting local specialities: *banh
beo, ram*, and *banh khoai*.

**Mme Ton Nu Ha's Tinh Gia
Vien Restaurant**, 20/3 Le
Thanh Ton Street, tel/fax:
(54) 522 243, e-mail:
tinhgiavien@dng.vnn.vn
Serves ten-course banquets
in the imperial style in a
garden setting. Presentation
is unique. Food is literally
sculpted by artist chef Mme
Ton Nu Ha. Vegetarian meals,
cookery classes on request.
Huong Giang Hotel,
tel: (54) 822 122. Serves good
Vietnamese and Western food
in its top-floor restaurant
overlooking the river. Its
ground floor restaurants stage

imperial banquets in costume
with traditional music.
Hue's Garden Houses, Huong
Giang Tourist Co., tel: (54) 832
221, fax: (54) 821 426, e-mail:
hgtravel@dng.vnn.vn Hue is
known for its gardens. Lunch,
sometimes dinner, can be
booked a day in advance with
a private tour.

Da Nang

Phi Lu Restaurant 2, 178
Nguyen Van Linh Street,
tel: (511) 650 039. Hanging
lamps, an arched bridge and
bird cages set the mood in
this highly praised Chinese
establishment.
Kim Do Restaurant, 182 Tran
Phu Street, tel: (511) 821 846.
More Chinese decor and a
vast Vietnamese and Chinese
menu, with a lot of seafood.

Hoi An

Hoi An Hai San, 64 Bach Dang
Street, tel: (510) 861 652. The
Tay family has been serving
excellent seafood for years in
this ideal spot for watching the
sun go down over the river.
Faifoo Restaurant, 104 Tran
Phu Street, tel: (510) 861 548.
A good place to order inex-
pensive Hoi An specialties.

SHOPPING

Hoi An

The **tailors** of Hoi An have
earned an international reputation – they are best at copying
clothes that fit. Hoi An also has
one of the best shopping streets
in Vietnam.

TOURS AND EXCURSIONS

Danang

Vidotour Danang, 760 Tran
Cao Van Street, Thanh Khe
District, tel: (511) 712 790,
fax: (511) 712 791, e-mail:
danang@vidotourtravel.com
www.vidotourtravel.com

Hue

Vidotour Hue, 18 Ly Thuong
Kiet Street, Hue,
tel: (54) 824 813, fax:
(54) 824 815, e-mail: hue@
vidotourtravel.com **Boat**
excursions to the imperial
tombs.
There are also excursions from
Hue to Vietnam War sites:
Sinh Café, 7 Nguyen Tri
Phuong Street, tel: (54) 824
813, e-mail: sinhcafetour@
hn.vnn.vn
Mandarin Café, 3 Hung
Vuong, tel: (54) 821 281,
e-mail: mandarin@dng.vnn.vn

Hoi An

Any hotel can arrange
excursions to **My Son**.

USEFUL CONTACTS

**Danang Family Medical
Practice**, 50–52 Nguyen Van
Linh Street, Nam Duong
Ward, Hai Chau District,
tel: (9) 13 917 303

HUE	J	F	M	A	M	J	J	A	S	O	N	D
AVERAGE TEMP. °F	70	72	75	79	82	84	84	84	87	78	75	71
AVERAGE TEMP. °C	21	21	24	26	28	29	29	29	27	26	24	22
HOURS OF SUN DAILY	4	5	3	7	9	8	9	7	6	5	4	4
RAINFALL in	3	1	1	1	2	3	3	4	14	24	14	8
RAINFALL mm	96	33	22	27	62	87	85	103	350	613	366	299
DAYS OF RAINFALL	14	7	5	6	9	8	9	4	15	21	21	19

5
Nha Trang and the Central Highlands

M ost people fly the 540km (337 miles) south from Da Nang to the beach resort of **Nha Trang**. You sacrifice some fine undeveloped beaches and a few Cham towers along the way, but it is easier to fly in, sit back and relax on the beach for a few days, and then think about excursions to the hill **tribes** of the Central Highlands (who still call themselves *montagnards*, as they were once referred to by the French).

In the past five years, Nha Trang has grown beyond all recognition from a sleepy fishing town with one idyllic resort and a dozen small hotels to a bustling beach town boasting over 100 hotels.

Vying with the **sea** for attention, however, are the **mountains**. Lying all along Vietnam's narrow coastal plain, the Truong Son Mountains make their presence felt. Although the **Central Highlands** are sparsely populated, the area has always been strategically important. Despite much of the hard wood forests having been either destroyed by Agent Orange during the Vietnam War or cleared for farming, a quarter of a century later, the lush greenness has now returned.

Buon Ma Thuot, north of Nha Trang (or fly to Buon Ma Thuot directly from Ho Chi Minh City), is the largest city in the western highlands and it lies in a coffee-growing area surrounded by a scattering of *montagnards* villages. Still further north, the town of Kon Tum itself contains certain neighbourhoods occupied by *montagnards*.

At the southern end of the Truong Son range, **Da Lat** is the hill station that the French playfully dubbed 'La Petite

Don't Miss

*** Nha Trang: *see* Cham towers and tropical beaches.
** Watersports: experience snorkelling and diving amongst the coral in Nha Trang.
* Hon Chong Promontory: visit this popular beauty spot near Nha Trang.
* Ngoan Muc Pass: capture vertiginous views on this panoramic mountain road.
** Da Lat: take a cool break in the highlands.

Opposite: *Sun, sea and sand – the palm-fringed beach of Nha Trang.*

CLIMATE

The climate is warmer, less humid and generally more tropical further south, except in the almost temperate Central Highlands, where it is cooler, even cold, from November to January. Unlike the rest of southern Vietnam, Nha Trang gets most of its rain during October and November. The rains, however, are rarely prolonged and usually limited to short, sharp spells, even during the wettest months. The dry season is from June to October.

Paris', a wonderful anomaly, complete with its own colourfully-lit Eiffel Tower. A favourite honeymoon destination of the Vietnamese, the town is built around a small lake, surrounded by a fertile upland region of rugged scenic beauty with forested hills, calm and enchanting lakes, and beautiful waterfalls.

NHA TRANG

A gently curving bay, a clear, warm turquoise sea and a superb beach of 6km (4 miles), plus a historical site or two, make Nha Trang the current most popular seaside destination in Vietnam. Five years ago Nha Trang felt like a big rustic village, with only one luxury beach resort and a dozen indifferent hotels.

Today the bumpy road along the beach has become a **boulevard** and a palm-lined **promenade**. On the beach you can get a massage, a pedicure or a beauty treatment. More than 100 hotels, a few luxurious, line the promenade and dot the streets inland. Several restaurants offer international cuisine. Nha Trang's population has soared to 322,000, and added to foreign visitors, the Vietnamese have discovered their own favourite beach resort.

Thanks to a huge fishing fleet of 10,000 trawlers in this region, Nha Trang is the **seafood** capital of Vietnam. On the northern side of town, beyond the new hotels facing

Below: *Market traders' rendezvous at an early morning fish market in Nha Trang.*

the beach, is another different Nha Trang – Nha Trang as Oriental fishing port. Take a stroll over the **Cai River Bridge** early in the morning and there are plenty of 'Kodak-moments' as the red and blue **fishing boats** come in from the night's fishing. Jostling for mooring space between the **stilt houses** that line the banks, the fishermen paddle to shore in their extraordinary round *thung chai* basket boats.

Beside the **Cai River Bridge**, Nha Trang has its own rather impressive Cham **monuments**, where

a steady stream of worshippers bearing offerings impart a very real sense of religious devotion.

NHA TRANG SIGHTS
Po Nagar Cham Towers

Known locally as **Thap Ba** (Lady of the City), these red brick towers, built between the 7th and 12th centuries, rise above the far bank of the Cai River, attractively sited on a flat hilltop overlooking the bridge and fishing harbour at the mouth of the river. Although the site has been used for Hindu worship since the 2nd century, the two principal towers honour the **Goddess of Po Nagar**, goddess of the Dua Liu clan, who ruled the southern region of the Cham Kingdom. The earliest wooden tower built on the site was burnt by the Javanese in AD774 and replaced by a brick and stone tower in AD784, the first of its kind. Of the original seven or eight towers, only four remain. The north tower, Thap Chinh, 23m (75 feet) high, was built in AD817. Inside is a black stone statue of the goddess Uma. The central tower, Thap Nam, built in the

12th century, holds a stone *linga* (a phallic symbol of male creation and Shiva). The south tower, Mieu Dong Ham, also houses a *linga*. The northwest tower, Thap Tay Bac, was originally devoted to Ganesha, the Hindu god represented by an elephant. The ten thick pillars to the right of the steps leading to the complex had originally supported the roof of a *mandala*, a resthouse for pilgrims. Now under reconstruction, the towers are a splendid example of Cham **architecture**, but what is more fascinating is that the site is still venerated.

Hon Chong Promontory
Not far beyond Po Nagar and off to the right, this promontory is a local beauty spot offering superb coastal views. There is a beach, but a nearby village renders it unsuitable for swimming.

Opposite: *Round basket boats sealed with tar, thung chai, ferry fisherman to shore in Nha Trang.*
Below: *A Cham religious sanctuary at Nha Trang, honouring Mother Goddess Po Nagar who is said to have taught local people new agricultural techniques.*

Long Song Pagoda
Look up anywhere in town and chances are you will glimpse an enormous white Buddha. Just west of the railway station (on 23 Thang 10 Street) stands the much renovated 19th-century Long Song Pagoda. The pagoda, topped with flamboyant glass and ceramic roof-ridge decoration, still has resident monks. Dominating the town from a nearby hill looms the 9m (30ft) white seated **Buddha**, defiantly erected in 1963 to commemorate the monks and nuns who died by self-immolation protesting the rule of South Vietnamese president Ngo Dinh Diem.

Nha Trang Cathedral
Returning towards the town centre, 23 Thang 10 Street leads into Thai Nguyen Street, at the end of which is the **cathedral**. Built in the 1930s on a small rock outcrop, this single-towered neo-Gothic building has a certain presence. Masses take place daily at 05:00 and 16:30.

Bao Dai's Villas
South of Nha Trang Beach, the land rises to a promontory occupied by Bao Dai's Villas. Built in the 1920s for the emperor, these five villas were later used by high-ranking

South Vietnamese officials as holiday homes, next by the newly powerful Northern government officials and today as tourist guesthouses. The stupendous view no doubt compensates for the mostly genuine period furnishings that would appeal to the highly romantic.

Cau Da

South of the headland is what used to be the muddy shore of a small fishing village, Cau Da. It has been developed as a modern quay serving a couple of dozen excursion boats waiting to take visitors to the islands. A new **aquarium** that defies credibility – the entrance to the ghostly Disney-like galleon that contains the aquarium is through the gargantuan mouth of a lion fish – has been built on a nearby island. At a fishing village on one of the islands, visitors are brought ashore in the tipsy round *thung chai* **basket boats**. New luxury resorts are mooted to be built on two of the islands. There is excellent snorkelling and scuba diving in the clear waters, of the surrounding bays offering a vast variety of designer tropical **fish** and delicate waving, living **corals**.

Excursions from Nha Trang
Doc Let Beach

Some consider this beach to be the most spectacular in Vietnam, long and wide with powder-white sand and shallow water. There are few visitors except at weekends. It lies on a peninsula 30km (18 miles) north of Nha Trang, past photogenic salt fields.

Central Highlights

Opposite: *Da Lat is the playground of Vietnamese honeymooners – there are boats to rent here.*

Buon Ma Thuot

Northwest of Nha Trang, 194km (116 miles) on a good – if steep – road, Buon Ma Thuot is the centre for visits to minority hill tribe villages (permits obtained from Dak Lak Tourist). The Ethnographic Museum – in part of what used to be another of Bao Dai's villas – at the corner of Nguyen Du and Le Duan Streets is open from Monday to Saturday (07:00–11:00 and 13:30–17:00). It displays artefacts of the 31 ethnic groups in Dac Lac Province. This is a **coffee** plantation area and you can buy coffee to take home at Nguyen Coffee Sales near the corner of Hai Ba Trung and Ama Trang Long. The rainy season is between April and November.

Yok Don National Park

Yok Don National Park is Vietnam's largest national park. The approach is via Ban Don Village northwest from Buon Ma Thuot. The **M'nong**, a matrilineal tribe that lives in the area, hunt wild elephants using domesticated **elephants**. Elephant rides must be booked through Dak Lak Tourist in Buon Ma Thuot. In the park are some 70 species of animals, 38 listed as endangered in Indo-China and 17 of those, worldwide, plus 200 species of birds. It takes a four-wheel-drive vehicle to reach Ban Don from Buon Ma Thuot, 45km (27 miles) away, or 148km (89 miles) north from Da Lat.

Kon Tum

About 246km (147 miles) north of **Buon Ma Thuot**, and 436km (262 miles) away from Nha Trang, lies Kon Tum, an awkward place to get to. It involves at least one overnight, but *montagnard* neighbourhoods literally ring the fringes of Kon Tum, making it unnecessary to have a permit.

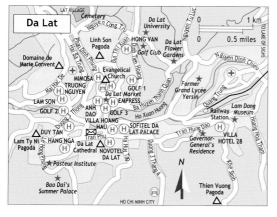

Da Lat

This Central Highlands hill resort lies 212km (132 miles) southwest of Nha Trang (or fly directly from Ho Chi Minh City – there are no flights from Nha Trang).The route heads first south along the coast down Highway 1 and then turns inland to Highway 11 at Phan Rang. Just off the road near Phan Rang

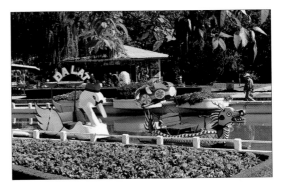

stand another couple of beautifully restored Cham towers. From here the road begins to climb the mountains in a series of startling switchbacks. At the highest point is **Ngoan Muc Pass** at 980m (3215ft), which the French called Bellevue Pass; the views are truly stunning, stretching out across the plain towards the coast.

Surviving the Vietnam War virtually unscathed, Da Lat remains today comparatively prosperous with a present population of about 160,000. On approaching the town, the villages seem neater, the children better dressed, and generally there is a feeling of greater spaciousness than what is found in the more densely populated lowlands.

Da Lat was created as a hill station in the early 20th century, following a visit to the area in 1897 by Dr Alexandre Yersin, the founder of the Pasteur Institute in Nha Trang. He thought the location, a hilly plateau at an elevation of 1475m (4839ft) above sea level, would make an ideal therapeutic retreat for Europeans suffering from the debilitating effects of lowland Vietnam's tropical climate.

The name Da Lat is a composite of two words: *da*, meaning 'water', and *Lat*, the name of a tribal people who have traditionally inhabited the region. The water of the lakes was an attraction for the French. The Lat were not and got shunted aside. By 1912, the hills surrounding the site's pleasant bowl-like depression

Da Lat Railway

From the 1930s until it was closed in 1964 due to a series of guerrilla attacks, a cog railway linked Da Lat to the coast. Today, Da Lat Railway Station is one of the town's curious little sights. A few kilometres of track have been reopened and railway enthusiasts can enjoy a jaunt into the Da Lat suburbs aboard a Russian-built diesel.

Da Lat Climate

Da Lat enjoys the unoriginal soubriquet 'City of Eternal Spring'. Throughout most of the year, days are bright and pleasantly warm and the nights cool, even cold in December and January. The rainy season is from May to November.

Above: *Da Lat's temperate climate encourages the cultivation of an abundance of exotic fruits and vegetables, which are artfully arranged on market stalls.*
Below: *The Central Highlands are home to a variety of ancient hilltribes – or montagnards – now struggling to maintain their unique way of life.*

had become dotted with European half-timbered villas that might have been lifted from Normandy to create a town that the French referred to affectionately, if incongruously, as 'Little Paris'.

With an average annual temperature of a very comfortable 18°C (65°F), the highland retreat earned a reputation as a salubrious spot. 'The pure bracing air stimulates the appetite', claimed a 1930s guidebook, 'and induces an inclination for physical exercise and brainwork, such as is never experienced at Saigon.' The area also had **agricultural** potential, and the temperate **climate** and fertile soil were suitable for cultivating a variety of cash crops such as vegetables, tea and coffee, and more recently grapes from which a very drinkable wine is now being produced. The strongest economic factor, however, is what it has always essentially been – **tourism** – and Da Lat is once again attracting thousands of Vietnamese tourists annually, especially honeymooners.

DA LAT SIGHTS

Perhaps because it was created as an escape, Da Lat draws much of its charm from an element of theatrical fantasy. The alpine woods, the neat villas, and a few veteran white Peugeot 203 taxis, all speak of elsewhere. Half the fun of sightseeing comes from simply wandering around the town's hillsides dotted with musty European-style villas and, like rummaging in someone's attic, marvelling at all the curious oddities.

For more specific sightseeing, Da Lat's focal point is **Xuan Huong Lake**, which lies in the southeastern part of the town. Created by damming the western end of the valley, the lake is quite pleasant with a couple of lake-side

restaurants. Paddle boats, some shaped like swans, are for hire. To the north are the **Da Lat Flower Gardens** with a robust display of orchids as well as temperate plants.

West of the lake's southern end and at the centre of the downtown area is the huge **Da Lat Market**. Built in the fifties, the main attractions are the stalls selling wood carvings, tribal baskets and weaving, tropical flowers and fruit, and a variety of teas.

Immediately northwest of Da Lat Market, continuing down the other side of the hill to Phan Dinh Phung Street, is an area for walking amid a townscape largely unchanged in appearance from the 1930s.

Da Lat Cathedral is located south of the town centre on Tran Phu Street near the Da Lat Palace Hotel. Built in the 1930s, this elegant building – with its single, shapely 47m (154ft) spire and French stained-glass windows – is a prominent landmark that sets historic Da Lat's quintessential Gallic tone.

Further religious landmarks are the **Domaine de Marie Convent**, now inhabited by a fraction of its once 300 nuns, easily recognizable for its tiled roofs and hilltop location on Ngo Quyen Street, and the pink-coloured **Evangelical Church** on Nguyen Van Troi Street.

Da Lat does not, for obvious reasons, boast venerable pagodas, although it has a few of interest. **Linh Son Pagoda**, on Phan Dinh Phung Street, about 1km (0.6 miles) north of the town centre, was founded in 1938 and is noted for its enormous bell, said to be cast of bronze and gold. **Quan Am Tu Pagoda** (Lam Ty Ni Pagoda), at 2 Thien My Street, is remarkable for one monk, Vien Thuc, who has worked tirelessly to develop the pagoda gardens; he is also a prolific painter. **Thien Vuong Pagoda**, sited on a pine-shaded hilltop on Khe Sanh Street about 4km (2.5 miles) southeast of town, is a Chinese temple known

> **PO KLONG GARAI TOWERS**
>
> Atop a small cactus-covered hill along the road to Da Lat, about 6km (4 miles) from Phan Rang, stands a group of four late 13th-century Cham towers. Purists may deplore their renovation, but silhouetted against the sky in their isolated location, they are impressive. An image of a dancing Siva can be seen over the main entrance to the biggest tower.

Below: *Beautiful orchids bloom in the Da Lat Flower Gardens.*

for its three huge gilded sandalwood statues. These statues are the largest in Vietnam and the centre one represents Sakyamuni, the Buddha of the Past.

Two secular buildings not to be missed are **Bao Dai's Summer Palace** and the **Governor-General's Residence**. They are both open daily (07:00–11:30 and 13:00–16:30). The former, set in attractive gardens about 2km (1.2 miles) southwest of the town centre on Le Hong Phong Street, is a big, airy 1930s villa complete with ornate throne and several portraits of the empress. The Governor-General's Residence, set on another hill, off Tran Hung Dao Street (the address of several large colonial villas) is of similar vintage and retains a certain stately air in its ambience (sometimes closed when in use for conferences).

AROUND DA LAT

The countryside around Da Lat is typified by pine-clad hills, rivers and waterfalls. Local beauty spots include the **Lake of Sighs** (Ho Than Tho), some 5km (3miles) northeast of town, and the **Valley of Love**, 5km (3 miles) north of Da Lat. Both have boating facilities. For the more energetic, Lang Bian Mountain, some 12km (7.5 miles) to the northwest, offers a three- to four-hour hike up a five-peak mountain, which tops 2000m (6560ft) and affords wonderful views.

Below: *Golf has now been added to Vietnam's visitor attractions.*

Lat Villages

Of nine hamlets, 12km (7 miles) north of Da Lat, five are inhabited by Lat ethnic people, the other three by Chill, Ma and Koho tribes, each speaking a different dialect. Lat houses are built on stilts and the villagers survive by growing rice, coffee, black beans and sweet potatoes. (Permits from Da Lat Toserco, 7 D 3 Thang 2).

Nha Trang and the Central Highlands at a Glance

October to **January** are the best months for most of Central Vietnam, when it is usually dry and cool, even cold, in the Central Highlands.

Nha Trang is served by **domestic flights** from Hanoi, Ho Chi Minh City and Da Nang. Vietnam Airlines also flies Ho Chi Minh City–Da Lat. The Hanoi–Ho Chi Minh City **railway** links Nha Trang with Hue and Da Nang. **Buses** arranged by tourist cafés are inexpensive and flexible.

Bicycles and **motorbikes** are easily rented from hotels and cafés. Da Lat is too hilly for *cyclos* (bicycle trishaws), but metered **taxis** and motorbike taxis are readily available in both Da Lat and Nha Trang.

Nha Trang
LUXURY
Ana Mandara Evason Resort & Six Senses Spa, Beachside Tran Phu Boulevard, tel: (58) 522 222, fax: (58) 525 828, e-mail: reservations-anamandara@evasonresorts.com Elegant beachside villas – one of the most exclusive resorts.
Yasaka-Saigon-Nha Trang Resort Hotel & Spa, 18 Tran Phu Blvd, tel: (58) 820 090, fax: (58) 820 000, e-mail: sg-nthotel@dng.vnn.vn www.yasanhatrang.com

MID-RANGE
Nha Trang Lodge, 42 Tran Phu Street, tel: (58) 521 500, fax: (58) 521 800, e-mail: nt-lodge@dng.vnn.vn Good value, high rise luxury in this Malaysian-Vietnamese hotel.

BUDGET
Vien Dong Hotel, 1 Tran Hung Dao, tel: (58) 523 606, fax: (58) 521 912, Comfortable hotel with a pool.

Da Lat
LUXURY
Hotel Sofitel Da Lat Palace, 12 Tran Phu Street, tel: (63) 825 444, fax: (63) 825 666, e-mail: sofitel@bdvn.vnd.net One of Asia's grand old hotels, but very pricey.
Novotel Da Lat, 7 Tran Phu Street, tel: (63) 825 777, fax: (63) 825 888, e-mail: novotel@bdvn.vnd.net Restored to modern comfort.

MID-RANGE
Empress Hotel, 5 Nguyen Thai Hoc Street, tel: (63) 833 888, fax: (63) 829 399, e-mail: empresdl@hcm.vnn.vn www.empresshotelvn.com

A tasteful new villa-style hotel overlooking the lake – excellent value and location.
Golf 3 Hotel, 4 Nguyen Thi Minh Khai Street, tel: (63) 826 042, fax: (63) 830 396, e-mail: golf3hot@hcm.vnn.vn The sleekest new effort of the local tourist authority.

BUDGET
Villa Huang Hau, 8A Ho Tung Mau Street, Ward 3, tel: (63) 821 431, fax: (63) 821 439. Scrupulously clean accommodation, with large, tiled-floored rooms, private baths with showers, just behind the Sofitel.

Nha Trang
Lac Canh Restaurant, 44 Nguyen Binh Khiem Street, tel: (58) 821 391. For 45 years this no-frills restaurant has been serving excellent seafood – try the marinated squid grilled at your table.

Nha Trang
Virtually all hotels organise trips to the islands and **diving**.

NHA TRANG	J	F	M	A	M	J	J	A	S	O	N	D
AVERAGE TEMP. °F	75	77	79	81	83	83	82	82	82	79	77	76
AVERAGE TEMP. °C	23	25	26	27	28	28	28	28	28	26	25	23
HOURS OF SUN DAILY	6	7	8	8	8	7	8	8	7	6	5	5
RAINFALL in	2	1	2	2	2	2	2	2	7	13	15	7
RAINFALL mm	47	17	52	53	55	49	43	51	167	326	376	167
DAYS OF RAINFALL	10	4	4	5	8	8	8	9	15	18	18	18

6
Ho Chi Minh City (Saigon)

Travelling south in Vietnam effectively means following the migratory route of the Viets as they pushed the Chams further and further south. Today the Chams are still clustered around Phan Rang situated on the coast south of Nha Trang, with a thin sprinkling in the Mekong Delta.

At 300 years old, **Ho Chi Minh City** is relatively young as a Vietnamese metropolis. It received an influx of Chinese immigrants in 1778 and in 1978 the reverse took place – an exodus with the introduction of anti-Chinese policies by the Hanoi government, confiscating Chinese property and assets.

Prior to the arrival of the French, Ho Chi Minh City was a trading settlement with one wooden fort. The French took control of the city in 1859, making it the capital of their southern colony, **Cochinchina**. With the French came stylish government buildings, a cathedral, broad boulevards and elegant villas – and even an opera house and baguettes.

During the **American War**, foreign correspondents filled the hotels and Ho Chi Minh City became the R & R capital of Vietnam for American troops. Drinking bars had flourished as well as prostitution and the city developed a reputation for tawdry sleaze. When the Americans left, the free-wheeling, free-for-all pre-1975 city had to change. With the arrival of new government officials from the north and the renaming of the city in 1978, Ho Chi Minh City was forced to develop a new, slightly less tarnished image. Today, once again, it thrives as the Vietnamese city, most pro-western, modern, sophisticated, trendy, and

DON'T MISS

★★★ History Museum: explore this splendid collection from all periods.
★★★ Reunification Palace: gain insight into modern history at what was once the Presidential Palace.
★★★ Giac Lam Pagoda: visit Saigon's oldest temple.
★★ Cao Dai temple: witness an unbelievable baroque extravaganza at Tay Ninh.
★★★ Mui Ne: experience this delightful small beach resort.
★★ Cu Chi Tunnels: sense a haunting reminder of war.

Opposite: *The hustle and bustle of the market in cosmopolitan Ho Chi Minh City.*

CLIMATE

Southern Vietnam experiences
two distinct seasons:
it is dry from November to
April and rainy from May to
October. The annual average
temperature is 27°C (80°F)
with a mean annual variation
of around 3°. The average
annual rainfall is 1900mm
(76in), while humidity
averages 79.5 per cent. The
wettest month is September
and the hottest is April. Ho
Chi Minh City boasts 2299
hours of sunshine a year.

entrepreneurial – its wheeler-dealer, free-for-all spirit
having been rapidly rejuvenated in the wake of the recent
economic liberalization.

With an official population figure of just under five million and rising, Ho Chi Minh City is Vietnam's largest city
and a major port, located on the western bank of the
Saigon River a few kilometres upstream from its outpour-
ing into the South China Sea. The city is the nation's hub
of revitalized commercial enterprise and exudes an almost
palpable air of confidence from behind the renovated
façades of hotels, new restaurants and bars. Hordes of
shiny new motorbikes snarl the streets. Shops and markets
are stocked with the latest imported technology, such as,
televisions, videos and computers.

Geographically, Ho Chi Minh City is 1700km (1062
miles) from **Hanoi** but since the *doi moi* (open door) policy
of 1988, encouraging foreign investment, the two cities
have been drawing closer and closer together and competing for investment capital, be it Australian, Japanese,
Korean, Taiwanese or American. In spite of all the
upheaval of recent decades, little has changed in the city's
original commercial aspirations.

Administratively, Ho Chi Minh City is divided into
12 urban districts (*quan*) and six suburban areas,
although the main tourist facilities are mostly contained
within the central District 1, lying between the river and
Le Duan Boulevard and focused around the parallel
streets of Nguyen Hue Boulevard and Dong Khoi Street.
The other main area of interest is **Cholon**, the old

Below: *River Saigon
which lies to the east of
the city.*

Chinatown, located a few streets to the
southwest. The riversideprovides additional
interest with small boats plying for trade
near the major hotels.

CITY SIGHTS

Central Ho Chi Minh City is a fairly compact
town and can be comfortably covered on
foot, although, *cyclos* hired by the hour are
always a pleasant way to travel, also provid-
ing an excellent view of the beautiful city.

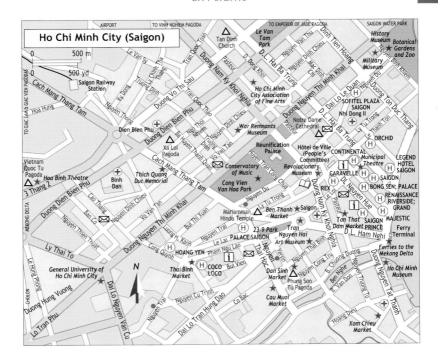

Ho Chi Minh City (Saigon)

The circuit up Nguyen Hue Boulevard, along the Le Loi Boulevard and down Dong Khoi Street makes a pleasant route, while on Sunday nights, it is the scene of the *chay rong rong* (literally, 'living fast'), an endless parade of hundreds of young people cruising on motorbikes, anxious to see and be seen.

Municipal Theatre *

Located on Dong Khoi, near the Continental and Caravelle hotels, the theatre was built in 1900 and was originally intended as a French opera house, although it lacks the architectural grandeur of its Hanoi counterpart. Transformed into South Vietnam's National Assembly in 1955, it is now once again a theatre staging anything from traditional **Vietnamese theatre** to modern pop groups. Performances at 20:00.

OFFICIAL TITLE

Although officially renamed Ho Chi Minh City after the 1975 Communist victory, the former capital of South Vietnam continues to be called Saigon by many local residents. The central area of the metropolis is, in fact, still properly referred to as Saigon.

MUSEUMS

History Museum, on Nguyen Binh Khiem. A fine collection of prehistoric, Cham and ethnic artefacts illustrating the numerous cultures of Vietnam. Open from Tuesday to Sunday (8:00–11.30 and 13:00–16:00).

War Remnants Museum, formerly the Museum of Chinese and American War Crimes, corner of Le Qui Don and Vo Van Tan. Horrific insights into the Vietnamese point of view on the war (open 7:30–11:45 and 13:30–16:45).

Museum of Ho Chi Minh City, formerly the Museum of the Revolution, 27 Ly Tu Trong Sreet. Exhibits in the former residence of the French governor of Cochinchina illustrating the Communist struggle. Open from Tuesday to Sunday (8:00–11.30 and 14:00–16:30).

Ho Chi Minh Museum, 1 Nguyen Tat Thanh Street, once the offices of a shipping company where Ho signed on as a ship's cook and left Vietnam in 1911. Open daily (7:30–11:30 and 13:30–21:00).

Fine Arts Museum, 97A Pho Dun Chinh Street, classical to social realism exhibits. Open from Tuesday to Sunday (7:45–11.30) and Monday to Saturday (13:30–16:15).

Hotel de Ville **

At the northwestern end of Nguyen Hue Boulevard, what was the City Hall under the French now houses the Ho Chi Minh City's **People's Committee**. A sunny, yellow-and-white gothic parody of the Hotel de Ville in Paris, it was constructed in the first years of the 20th century and is remarkable for the incongruity of its ornate European **architecture** set in the middle of an Asian city. Probably the most photographed building in town, it stands across the street from a statue of **Ho Chi Minh** in a small park where old men play draughts (checkers).

Notre Dame Cathedral **

Standing in a square at the top of Dong Khoi Street is the red-brick, neo-Romanesque Catholic cathedral built by the French between 1877 and 1883. With imposing twin towers and an attractive interior, the entrance to **Notre Dame** is dominated by a statue of the **Virgin Mary** – its stained glass windows were a casualty of World War II.

General Post Office *

On the eastern side of the square stands the French-built post office dating from the 1880s. Its splendid colonial-style **architecture** somehow resembles a European railway station more than a post office.

Reunification Palace ***

Also known as the **Thong Nhat Conference Hall**. Situated on the south of the cathedral along Nguyen Du Street stands what was the **Presidential Palace** prior to 1975. In an image from a famous press photograph that came to symbolize the fall of Ho Chi Minh City (Saigon), a North Vietnamese tank crashes through the main gates of the Palace (30 April 1975). The original 19th-century building that occupied the site was the residence of the **French governor**. In 1962, two Vietnamese air force pilots bombed the building in a vain attempt to assassinate **President Diem**. The partially destroyed building was then pulled down and a new palace built. The exterior is typical of 1960s architecture, while inside are a conference hall, banquet hall and meeting rooms of stately proportions, the private apartments of the president and an underground operations centre.

War Remnants Museum *

It is close to the Reunification Palace, at 28 Vo Van Tan Street, and presents a largely photographic display (there is some hardware on show, ranging from a turn-of-the-century French guillotine to captured American weaponry) of man's **inhumanity** to man, predictably much of it US initiated during the war. Although grisly and sobering, it is a compelling **tourist attraction**. The museum is open daily (7:30–11:45 and 13:30–16:45).

History Museum ***

Open daily except on Mondays (8:00–11.30 and 13:00–16:00) and situated at the north end of Le Duan Boulevard, at Nguyen Binh Khiem Street, in the grounds of the **Botanical Gardens and Zoo**, this museum should not be missed. Housed in an imposing 1920s building of what could be called neo-Vietnamese architecture is a fine collection of **sculpture**, **pottery** and other artefacts from all major **historical periods**, from the Bronze Age Dong Son civilization through the Funan, Chenla, Khmer and Cham periods, the various minorities and Vietnamese dynastic eras.

HO CHI MINH CITY PAGODAS

Ho Chi Minh City has far more pagodas than a brief visit could possibly encompass. Some of the best are in Cholon (see page 103). The following is a shortlist of the most striking:

Emperor of Jade
(Ngoc Hoang) Pagoda ***

Dating from the turn of the century, this atmospheric pagoda, at 73 Mai Thi Luu Street, north of Dien Bien

---

TRAN HUNG DAO

Although Ho Chi Minh City wasn't on the map when Tran Hung Dao repelled a Mongol invasion in 1287, the national hero is well remembered in the city. A robust statue of a fearsome-looking Tran Hung Dao stands in Hero Square facing the river, while a temple dedicated to the general, at 34 Vo Thi Sau Street, has bas-reliefs depicting his exploits.

Below: *East meets West – the Hotel de Ville provides a European backdrop to a typically Asian scene.*

Above: *Imposing temple architecture is softened by muted pink exteriors.*

Phu Street just before the Thi Nghe Channel, blends **Taoism** and **Buddhism** in its dedication to various Chinese and Vietnamese divinities – the Emperor of Jade is the supreme god of the Taoists. In addition to the temple's statuary and rich ornamentation, the **Hall of Ten Hells** is noted for its carved wooden panels depicting the torments that await the ungodly. **Prayers**, chanting with drums, bells and gongs, take place at 4:00 and 11:00 and 16:00 and 19:00.

Giac Lam Pagoda ★★★
Dating from 1774, this is probably Ho Chi Minh City's oldest pagoda. Located in the western part of the city in Tan Binh District at 118 Lac Long Quan Street, the pagoda is enormously appealing for its traditional architecture, decoration and numerous statues, funerary tablets and other religious artefacts. The compound holds a sacred *bodhi* tree from Sri Lanka.

Giac Vien Pagoda ★★★
In District 11 southwest of the city, next to Dam Sen Lake at 247 Lac Long Quan Street, Giac Vien is similar in style and atmosphere to Giac Lam Pagoda. Giac Vien's main attraction is its superbly carved **statues** of Buddha and other divinities.

Vinh Nghiem Pagoda ★★
At 339 Nam Ky Khoi Nghia Street in District 3 (north-west of the central area), this is a modern pagoda, completed in 1973 with aid from the Japan-Vietnam Friendship Association. It has the distinction of being Ho Chi Minh City's largest pagoda. The architectural style is

Japanese influenced and the most dominant feature is a classic seven-storey tower with statues of the **Buddha** on every level. Two fierce warriors guard the pagoda entrance. Behind the large sanctuary is a three-storey funeral tower containing burial urns.

Xa Loi Pagoda *

At 89 Ba Huyen Thanh Quan Street, near Dien Bien Phu Street in District 3 (northwest of Reunification Palace), Xa Loi Pagoda offers more **historical** than aesthetic interest. Built in 1956, the pagoda became a famous centre of protest against the regime of President Diem and in August 1963, it was violently **raided** by armed government forces. The incident served to consolidate Buddhist opposition to Diem and several monks committed self-immolation at the pagoda in protest. Of note among the pagoda buildings is a multi-tiered tower that enshrines a relic of the **Buddha**.

CHOLON

Comprising District 5, southwest of central Ho Chi Minh City, Cholon is the original **Chinese town**, built at the end of the 18th century. The name translates as 'Big Market' and the district, like Chinatowns elsewhere, is a commercial area, a hive of entrepreneurial activity with family businesses conducted from little shophouses packed cheek-by-jowl in bustling, narrow streets.

In spite of thousands of Chinese fleeing Vietnam as a result of the discriminatory government policies in the late seventies, Cholon retains its quintessential Chinese flavour. Highlights are the Chinese **pagodas**, whose tiled roofs and typically flamboyant decoration break the urban monotony. The following sights are within easy walking distance of one another.

HO CHI MINH CITY SHOPPING

Shopping in Ho Chi Minh City can be rewarding. The best buys are concentrated in the Dong Khoi Street area. Antique-cum-junk shops offer a few lucky finds, especially Chinese and Vietnamese ceramics, but check on export restrictions. Otherwise contemporary paintings are a good buy, as is silk, while lacquerware and inlaid mother-of-pearl boxes can be found almost anywhere.

Below: *With its narrow streets, Cholon appears to be the busiest, noisiest and most heavily populated part of Ho Chi Minh City.*

MARKETS

In the southern part of downtown, the city's largest market is Ben Thanh, which sells everything from fresh produce to clothes and toys. Built in 1914 and covering 11,000m² (118,400 square feet), it is a fascinating place for browsing, but beware of pickpockets. Binh Tay in Hau Giang Blvd is Cholon's main market, full of evocative sights, scenes, sounds, colours and smells. Cholon's newer five-storey market is An Dong, near the intersection of Tran Phu and An Duong Vuong Boulevards, first opened in 1991.

Thien Hau Pagoda ★★★

This pagoda, at 710 Nguyen Trai Street, dates from the early 19th century and is Cholon's largest and one of its busiest pagodas. It is dedicated to Thien Hau, **Goddess of the Sea**, and in addition to its statuary and other usual religious furnishings, the pagoda is remarkable for the richly detailed ceramic **friezes** decorating the roof.

Nghia An Hoi Quan Pagoda ★★

At 678 Nguyen Trai Street, the temple is dedicated to legendary Chinese warrior Quan Cong, whose glass-encased statue is at the main altar flanked by those of his companions, General Chau Xuong (on the left) and the Mandarin Quan Binh. A gilded carved wooden boat hangs over the entrance and, to the left, huge figures of Quan Cong's horse and groom.

Quan Am Pagoda ★★★

Located at 12 Lao Tu Street, the early 19th-century Quan Am Pagoda is another excellent example of typical Chinese pagoda architecture and ornamentation with multiple **courtyards** and a profusion of variously dedicated **altars**. Note the ceramic tableaux used as roof decoration, the beautiful gilded and lacquered door panels and **statues** including figures of A-Pho, the Holy Mother, and Quan Am, Goddess of Mercy, by the main altar and to the left, Dia Tang Vuong Bo Tat, the King of Hell.

Below: *Light and dark: inside Nghia An Hoi Quan Pagoda.*

Tam Son Hoi Quan Pagoda ★★

At 118 Trieu Quang Phuc Street, childless mothers come to pray at this 19th-century pagoda dedicated to Me Sanh, the Goddess of Fertility. The pagoda also displays statues of General Quan Cong and his horse and Thien Hau, Goddess of the Sea.

Cha Tam Church ★

Lying west of the above-mentioned cluster of pagodas at the end of Tran Hung Dao Boulevard, is the church where **President Ngo Dinh Diem** and his brother were **arrested** and **assassinated** in the coup of November 1963.

DAY EXCURSIONS FROM HO CHI MINH CITY
Cu Chi Tunnels **

On the way to Tay Ninh some 35km (22 miles) northwest of Ho Chi Minh City, the tunnels are an amazing concept rather than an arresting sight. What visitors see today is a small, somewhat enlarged, section of a 200km (125 miles) network of interconnected and multi-storey

underground passages averaging 1.5m (5ft) high and 0.7m (2ft) wide, which served as a huge subterranean Viet Cong base. Here, literally under the feet of the **US forces** who had a base in Cu Chi district, were **Communist** command posts, field hospitals, weapons factories, classrooms and living quarters.

All hand dug, the tunnels were begun by the **Viet Minh** in the forties as part of the struggle against the **French**. The underground system was then renovated and extended by the Viet Cong in the sixties when the war with the USA escalated. Although the Americans eventually discovered the existence of the tunnels, they could never ultimately destroy them, in spite of employing a special volunteer force of 'tunnel rats'. The full story is related in the book, *The Tunnels of Cu Chi*, by Tom Mangold and John Penycate.

A 50m (164ft) section of the tunnels is open to visitors and even these enlarged passages can induce claustrophobia. The visitors' centre displays a wall map showing the full extent of the underground system and tour guides give a brief history of the tunnels and a description of the conditions endured here by the Viet Cong.

Tay Ninh ***

Lying close to the Cambodian border 96km (60 miles) northwest of Ho Chi Minh City, Tay Ninh is often combined with Cu Chi on a full-day excursion. The small

Above: *All roads in Ho Chi Minh City seem eventually to lead to a market. Starting out as a trading settlement, Ho Chi Minh City continues to place importance on material persuits.*

TEMPLE ETIQUETTE

Visitors to the Cao Dai Temple at Tay Ninh should not enter the central portion of the nave, nor should they wander in and out during services. It is also disrespectful for visitors to leave before a service has ended. Services usually last about one hour.

Above: *The only sand dunes in Vietnam rise well back from the sea, north of Mui Ne.*

provincial town is famous as the site of the Great Temple of the Cao Dai religion, one of Vietnam's home-grown faiths.

Dating from the 1930s, this Cao Dai 'cathedral' and headquarters of the religion stands amid a well-ordered complex of administrative buildings, residences and a hospital of herbal medicine. There is no mistaking the Great Temple itself, a yellow-painted, twin-towered baroque extravaganza, part European church, part Vietnamese pagoda. Even more dazzling is the eye-catching multi-coloured interior, where dragon-entwined columns and other typically exuberant Oriental-style ornamentation, compounded by Cao Dai symbolism, have a kaleidoscopic effect. It is not to everyone's taste. Travel writer Norman Lewis, on a visit in 1950, thought the Great Temple 'must be the most outrageously vulgar building ever to have been erected with serious intent. It was a palace in candy from a coloured fantasy by Disney; an example of fun-fair architecture in extreme form'.

It can be truly overwhelming, but it is probably the single most unforgettable building in the whole of Vietnam. Services at the Great Temple are held daily at 6:00, noon, 18:00 and midnight. With priests dressed in bright red, blue or yellow robes, the ceremonies are colourful affairs. Visitors are allowed and unobtrusive photography is permitted.

Around Ho Chi Minh City

Mui Ne Beach (Phan Thiet) ★★★
Vung Tau, previously known as **Cap St Jacques** by the French, may be the nearest beach to Ho Chi

Minh City, but as it is on the delta near a refinery, it is not the most appealing. For powdery white sand and swaying palms, the nearest resort on the South China Sea is at **Phan Thiet** (the town), 200km (125 miles) from Ho Chi Minh City. The beach, **Mui Ne**, starts 11km (7 miles) further on. It is easily reached on a good road (Route 1 to Phan Thiet, then Route 706 to Mui Ne) in about four hours by car or bus through Ho Chi Minh City tourist cafés.

Mui Ne is a long stretch, 10km (6 miles) of white sandy beach along a peninsula, a newish **resort** of some 15–20 small, tasteful, mostly family-owned hotels that have been built since 1995. They are generally (air-conditioned) bungalows scattered amongst tropical gardens around a pool, facing the sea. Here you can step off the terrace of your bungalow onto the beach (a great way to recuperate from jetlag and see Ho Chi Minh City later).

The international hotel chains have yet to arrive (exceptions are Novotel and EEM) – in short, a real find at an agreeable stage of small-scale development.

Apart from lazing on the beach or by the pool, a couple of Cham towers, some rather spectacular sand dunes just north of town, a floating village of fishermen and a village producing *nuoc mam* (Vietnam's all purpose seasoning sauce made from fermented fish), may entice you out the hammock, briefly.

Approximately 40 minutes south, 28km (17 miles), on top of **Takou Mountain**, lies Vietnam's largest reclining Buddha at 49m (159ft) long – at the end of a 90-minute climb.

Rainy months are July, August and September. High season is December and January. Around **Tet**, rooms can be tightly booked, but it is a great place to drop off and sleep to the sound of the sea.

> **TRIPS INTO THE INTERIOR**
>
> Nui Ba Den, or Black Lady Mountain, is the highest point in southern Vietnam, rising to nearly 1000m (3280ft) above the surrounding plain 15km (9 miles) northeast of Tay Ninh. It has long been a sacred site and the mountain is dotted with cave temples. A stiff climb up is rewarded by fine panoramic views. The mountain's name is derived from the legend of a woman who threw herself off the peak instead of surrendering her honour to a gang of kidnappers. In real life, Nui Ba Den was the scene of fierce fighting during both the First and Second Indo-China Wars.

Below: *Mui Ne beach near Phan Thiet, east of Ho Chi Minh City.*

Ho Chi Minh City (Saigon) at a Glance

BEST TIMES TO VISIT

Ho Chi Minh City is most comfortable from **December** through **February** with average temperatures between 20°C and 25°C (68–77°F).

GETTING THERE

Ho Chi Minh City's airport, Tan Son Nhat, is a 20- to 30-minute taxi ride from the city; be sure to get a metered taxi. Customs and arrival formalities can be tedious. Once through, facilities include money exchange, post office and a tourism information desk. Ho Chi **Minh City Railway Station** is in District 3, about 2km (1.25 miles) from the city centre at 1 Nguyen Thong Street, tel: (8) 823 0105. Use **buses** organized by tourist cafés (local tour operators), or a **car** and **driver**.

GETTING AROUND

The typical way of getting around Ho Chi Minh City is by **cyclo**. Sitting facing oncoming traffic can be a trifle unnerving at first, but the vantage point really does offer an excellent view of the city (take **taxis** after dark). There are taxi stands outside the main tourist hotels. For those brave enough, **motorcycle taxis** can be flagged in the street. Hire **cars** (with driver) are readily available from the main hotels and tour companies, while **bicycles** or **motorbikes** can be hired from budget hotels. Local buses are not recommended

WHERE TO STAY

Ho Chi Minh City (Saigon)
Ho Chi Minh City has a few excellent hotels and a wide selection of comfortable mid-range and inexpensive hotels. Best rates are often negotiated through an agent.

LUXURY
Caravelle Hotel, 19 Lam Son Square, District 1, tel: (8) 823 4999, fax: (8) 824 3999, e-mail: hotel@caravellehotel.vnn.vn A luxurious new tower has been added to this renovated colonial hostelry opposite the Opera House. A pool and a nostalgic rooftop bar.
Legend Hotel Saigon, 2-4A Ton Duc Thang, tel: (8) 823 3333, fax: (8) 823 2333, e-mail: info@legendhotelsaigon.com www.legendsaigon.com Life-sized bronze horses and a fountain set the style of this smooth, riverside tower.
Renaissance Riverside, 8–15 Ton Duc Thang, tel: (8) 822 0033, fax: (8) 823 5666, website: www.marriot.com Another ultra-modern luxury hotel on the Saigon River.
Sofitel Plaza Saigon, 17 Le Duan Blvd, District 1, tel: (8) 824 1555, fax: (8) 824 1666, e-mail: sofsgn-resa@hcmc.net nam.vn www.wofitel.com A French Accor group hotel located near Notre Dame Cathedral and consulates.
Equatorial Hotel, 242 Tran Binh Trong Street, Dist 5, tel: (8) 839 7777, fax: (8) 839 0011, e-mail: info@hcm. equatorial.com

Modern luxury, host to numerous heads of state, located between the centre and Cholon (Chinatown).

MID-RANGE
Hotel Majestic, 1 Dong Khoi Street, tel: (8) 829 5517, fax: (8) 829 5510, e-mail: majestic@majesticsaigon.com.vn www.majesticsaigon.com.vn Long-time favourite; grand old-fashioned art-deco elegance overlooking the Saigon river.
Rex Hotel, 141 Nguyen Hue Boulevard, tel: (8) 829 2185, fax: (8) 829 6536, e-mail: rexhotel@hcm.vnn.vn www.rexhotelvietnam.com Indochine nostalgia, a long established hotel (full of cane and rattan), with a kitch bar.
Continental, 132 Dong Khoi Street, tel: (8) 829 9201 , fax: (8) 829 0936, e-mail: info@continental-saigon.com www.continentalvietnam.com Good enough for Graham Green and Jacques Chirac, beautifully renovated colonial style. Central, but no pool.
Grand Hotel, 8 Dong Khoi, District 1, tel: (8) 823 0163, fax: (8) 823 5781, e-mail: grandsgn@grandhotel.com.vn www.grandhotel.com.vn The renovated colonial wing is dearer than the new.

BUDGET
Bong Sen, 17–123 Dong Khoi, District 1, tel: (8) 829 1516, fax: (8) 829 8076, e-mail: bongsen1@hcm.vnn.vn www.hotelbongsen.com Big rooms with sofas, famous restaurant buffets, central.

Ho Chi Minh City (Saigon) at a Glance

Palace Hotel, 56–64 Nguyen Hue, District 1, tel: (8) 829 2860, fax: (8) 824 4230, e-mail: palace@hcm.vnn.vn Good value in shopping area, some rooms with balconies.

Mui Ne beach (Phan Thiet)
LUXURY

Victoria Phan Thiet Resort, Km 9 Phu Hai, tel: (62) 813 000/2/3/4/5, fax: (62) 813 007, e-mail: resa.phanthiet@ victoriahotels-asia.com www.victoriahotels-asia.com Rustic style luxury bungalows in bougainvillaea and orchid gardens on the sea.

Novotel Ocean Dunes & Golf Resort, 1 Ton Duc Thang Street, Phan Thiet, tel: (62) 822 393, fax: (62) 825 682 e-mail: novpht@accorhotels-asia.com Pricey four-star resort; Nick Faldo designed the golf course.

MID-RANGE
Coco Beach Resort, 58 Nguyen Dinh Chieu, Ward Ham Tien, tel: (62) 847 111/2/3/4, fax: (62) 847 115, e-mail: paradise@cocobeach.net www.cocobeach.net French-German owned, wooden bungalows in tropical gardens on the beach. Restaurant serving French cuisine Tue–Sun.

Swiss Village Resort, Km 12 Ham Tien, tel: (62) 847 480, fax: (62) 847 491, e-mail: SVR.Reservation.02@vnn.vn www.svr-vn.com New oriental-style bungalows in gardens with a tea house.

BUDGET
Full Moon, 84 Nguyen Dinh Chieu, Ham Tien, tel: (62) 847 008, fax: (62) 847 160, e-mail: fullmoonwindsurf-vietnam@ yahoo.com Inexpensive bungalow and villa rooms, thatched restaurant by the sea.

WHERE TO EAT

Highly rated favourites include: **Mandarin**, 11A Ngo Van Nam, District 1, tel: (8) 822 9783. Locals consider this the best, if pricey, Vietnamese food. **Indochine Saigon**, 32 Pham Ngoc Thach, District 3, tel: (8) 823 9256. Gourmet Vietnamese food in elegant colonial villa and garden. **Hoi An**, 11 Le Thanh Ton, District 1, tel: (8) 823 7694. Elegant Vietnamese style food. **The Temple Club**, 29 Ton That Thiep Street, District 1, tel: (8) 829 9244. Good Vietnamese food in clubby 1930s style sitting room.

Brodard Café & Restaurant, 1 Nguyen Thiep, District 1, tel: (8) 822 3966. A convenient long-standing institution serving good French food. **Augustin**, 10 Nguyen Thiep Street, tel: (8) 829 2941. Inexpensive bistro-type food.

Sesame, 153 Xo Viet Nghe Tinh, Binh Thanh District, tel: (8) 899 3378. A hospitality training school for orphans.

TOURS AND EXCURSIONS

Day tours are more developed in Ho Chi Minh City than elsewhere. The pioneer in the field, state-run profit-earning Saigon Tourist, has now been joined by other private companies – whose prices are cheaper. **Vidotour**, 145 Nam Ky Khoi Nghia Street, District 3, tel: (8) 933 0457, fax: (8) 933 0470, e-mail: info@vidotourtravel.com www.vidotourtravel.com **Sinh Cafe**, 248 De Tham, District 1, tel: 836 9420, fax: (8) 836 9322, e-mail: info@ sinhcafe.com **Kim Travel**, 270 De Tham, District 1, tel: (8) 920 5552/3, fax: (8) 836 9859 e-mail: cafekim@hcm.vnn.vn www.kimtravel.com

USEFUL CONTACTS

HCMC Family Medical & Dental Practice, Diamond Plaza, 34 Le Duan Street, District 1, tel: (8) 822 7848, Japanese tel: (8) 822 1919.

HO CHI MINH CITY	J	F	M	A	M	J	J	A	S	O	N	D
AVERAGE TEMP. °F	78	80	83	85	83	82	80	80	81	80	79	79
AVERAGE TEMP. °C	26	27	28	29	28	28	27	27	27	27	26	26
HOURS OF SUN DAILY	8	8	9	8	7	6	6	6	5	6	7	7
RAINFALL in	0	0	0	2	9	12	12	11	13	10	5	2
RAINFALL mm	14	4	10	50	218	312	293	270	327	266	117	48
DAYS OF RAINFALL	2	1	2	5	18	22	23	22	23	21	12	7

7
The Mekong Delta

One would never imagine, standing in the midst of Ho Chi Minh City's snarling traffic, that hardly an hour away from this burgeoning metropolis is the intensely rural **Mekong Delta**, a green, watery realm that is quint-essentially Vietnamese. The vast flatlands of this liquid maze make up Vietnam's 'rice bowl', and the towns of the delta act as little more than service stations to a rather sprawled patchwork of rice paddies criss-crossed by rivers, streams and canals.

Roads connecting the principal towns are surprisingly good and, seemingly, constantly being improved – the new $35m **Friendship Bridge** between Ha Tien and My Tho, a joint venture between Australia and Vietnam, eliminates a time-consuming ferry. Hotel accommodation is relatively simple, with two notable exceptions. There are no major tourist sights in the delta and nor do the cities hold much appeal. Rather it is the delta itself and the people who live in this watery environment that fascinate the visitor.

EXPLORING THE MEKONG DELTA

Covering slightly more than 3.7 million ha (9 million acres), from the air the delta looks like a great green carpet interlaced by the silvery threads of countless streams and canals. Thrusting through the green are the thick brown fingers of the **Mekong** and its tributary, the **Bassac** (known in Vietnamese, respectively, as the Tien and the Hau, the 'upper' and 'lower' rivers), which flow roughly 200km (125 miles) from Vietnam's border with Cambodia to the

DON'T MISS

*** My Tho: a delightful delta port within easy reach of Ho Chi Minh City.
*** Can Tho: explore the unofficial delta capital with its own lively floating market.
*** Chau Doc: see an attractive commercial centre with numerous floating houses.
** Sam Mount: witness a rare elevation near Chau Doc covered with an assortment of religious buildings.
* Tan Long Island: enjoy this pretty island retreat noted for its longan orchards.

Opposite: *On the waterfront – a typical delta home, raised on stilts to offset the risk of flooding.*

South China Sea. Estuary islands further divide the mainstreams that then fan out in a classic delta pattern, finally flowing into the sea from eight mouths. But eight is an unlucky number, so the Vietnamese count one more small channel, thus giving the river its local name, **Cuu Long Giang** – meaning River of Nine Dragons.

Transforming the land between the streams into a watery maze is an intricate web of **canals**, some short and narrow, others long, wide highways – running as straight as a die 50km (30 miles) – and more to link the Bassac with the **Gulf of Thailand**. No one knows exactly the combined length of these waterways, although estimates put it close to 5000km (3125 miles) – nearly 1000km (625 miles) longer than the entire course of the Mekong River.

Ranging over nine administrative provinces, the Mekong Delta is flat – any spot above 5m (16ft) is quite rare – but it is not featureless. Topographical diversity is found in the **Plain of Reeds**, an extensive low-lying area in the north where 'floating' rice copes with the swampy conditions, and in the **U-Minh forest** on the Ca Mau peninsula to the south.

Wrested from the Khmer only in the 18th century, the Mekong Delta is the newest part of Vietnam. It is nonetheless of vital importance as the country's single largest tract of arable land. Today, 45 per cent of Vietnam's total **rice** output comes from the delta. Also

Right: *The Mekong Delta is laced in a network of canals dug to expand rice cultivation. A milder climate for the crop than in the Red River Delta enables the region to produce three crops annually.*

Left: *Characterized by its flatness, any elevation is unusual in the delta region.*

cultivated in significant quantities are **soya beans**, **maize**, **sorghum**, **peanuts**, **pineapples**, **sugar cane** and **coconut palms**, as well as **orchard fruits**.

The delta's calm, bucolic appearance belies what has at times been a rather violent past. From the days of the Nguyen lords, it was an area of **conquest**, **settlement**, and later resettlement as populations were shifted in the periodic upheavals of Vietnam's turbulent history. This factor, combined with the delta's economic significance, made the region, somewhat frequently, a hotbed of social **unrest**, fuelled by the iniquities of oppressive land-lords. Here were warlords, river pirates and, lastly, communist insurgents.

During the **Vietnam War** the swampy flatlands were a stronghold of the Viet Cong and the area saw some of the most vicious fighting under the worst possible physical conditions. To quote an article published in *National Geographic* in 1968, 'War, on any battle-field is a nightmare. The Mekong Delta compounds the horror. To fight here means tortuous slogging through snake-ridden swamps, where sucking mud grips the legs like wet

CLIMATE

Between January and March the temperature in the Mekong Delta ranges between 22°C and 34°C (72°F and 93°F). The humidity and rainfall increase from May onwards, and the wettest months are between July and October. During this time, flooding may occur, which can restrict travel.

Above: *Ploughing fields the traditional way near My Tho.*

concrete. The enemy may be only five feet away, yet unseen in the thick jungle.'

Today, with the fertile delta once again flourishing, it is hard to believe that modern warfare once turned this placid countryside into a nightmare.

Although overwhelmingly **rural**, the Mekong Delta does have several large **towns** – Can Tho has a population of 330,000, Long Xuyen 238,000, My Tho 169,000, and Vinh Long 124,000. These and other less important centres are sited along the main river channels, most often where intersected by major transportation canals. **Rach Gia**, (with a population of 172,000) on the Gulf of Thailand, is the only significant town on the sea coast.

The homogeneity of the delta – the population is overwhelmingly Vietnamese with a sprinkling of Khmer Krom (southern Khmer), Chinese and Cham – is contrasted by an amazing diversity of religious practice. Encountered within surprising proximity are more places of worship of different persuasion than perhaps any other rural area in the world – **Buddhist** temples of both the Theravada and Mahayana persuasions, **Catholic** churches, **Muslim** mosques, **Cao Dai** temples and **Chinese** shrines to various minor deities all add fascination to the charm of the surroundings.

Apart from the rural landscape and the region's religious mosaic, the other attraction of travelling through the delta is the early morning floating **markets**, typically held at the junction of two or more main canals.

To minimise the cost of boats, the easy way to explore the Delta is via the well-organised **tours** from Ho Chi Minh City. A wide variety are on offer from a one-day taster tour to My Tho, to three- or four-day tours around Can Tho and Chau Doc, and many more that are longer and further afield.

MY THO

The closest Mekong town to Ho Chi Minh City and one of the most charming of the delta ports, **My Tho** lies 70km (45 miles) southwest of the metropolis in an area noted for its **rice paddies** and **fruit orchards**. The capital of Tien Gian Province, the town lies at a right angle formed by the junction of the Bao Dinh Channel and the northernmost branch of the Mekong. One of My Tho's greatest pleasures is simply to while away an hour or two in a café watching the **aquatic** world slip by or, better still, join it on a boat tour.

The narrow canals around My Tho are crossed by tiny wooden and bamboo bridges. The banks are fringed by water palms whose graceful fronds form green arches. These narrow canals are some of the most beautiful in the entire delta. Only five minutes away, **Tan Long** is a pretty little island, famous for its **longan orchards** (longans are related to lychees). **Phung Island**, about 20 minutes by boat, once held the open-air sanctuary of a small religious sect headed by the 'Coconut Monk'. Reputedly, monks were allowed nine wives, adding considerably to its attraction as a religion. Now visitors are shown a coconut candy 'factory'.

ISLAND OF THE COCONUT MONK

About 3km (2 miles) from My Tho, **Phung Island** was established as a retreat by the 'Coconut Monk' at the end of World War II. Ong Dao Dua, a charismatic leader, initiated a new religion that fused Buddhist and Christian elements. For three years he is said to have sat and meditated on a stone slab, sustained only by a diet of coconuts (hence the nickname). His philosophy advocated peaceful reunification of the country, for which he suffered persecution both by the South Vietnamese government and subsequently the communists.

Left: *A fisherman's houseboat: to the people of the Mekong Delta, the river provides both a living and a home. Fishing and rice-growing are the main economic activities of the region, although tourism is becoming increasingly popular.*

U-MINH FOREST

The world's largest mangrove swamp outside the Amazon covers some 1000km² (386 square miles) of the Ca Mau peninsula, Vietnam's south-ernmost tip comprising the Mekong Delta province of Minh Hai. The area is well off the tourist track, although the town of Ca Mau, 179km (112 miles) southwest of Can Tho, provides basic facilities. U-Minh suffered severe damage from chemical defoliants during the Vietnam War and in spite of some recovery, remains under threat from local encroachment. An intriguing area for the natural-ist or conservationist.

Tourist sights in My Tho include **Vinh Trang Pagoda**, a short distance from the town centre at 60A Nguyen Trung Truc Street, a delightful 19th-century pagoda with a wooden interior concealed behind a colonial façade added in 1907. **My Tho's Central Market**, a length of market stalls strung along Trung Truc and Nguyen Hue Streets, presents a lively, local scene. **My Tho Catholic Church**, located on the corner of Hung Vuong Boulevard and Nguyen Trai Street, is a pleasant yellow-washed church dating from the late 19th century, serving a size-able Catholic population.

VINH LONG

Capital of the province of the same name, **Vinh Long** is situated on the Mekong River some 65km (40 miles) southwest of My Tho. The town is little more than a pit-stop on the journey between My Tho and Can Tho; **boats** can be hired here for **excursions**. One possible excursion is by narrow wooden boat poled along metre-wide canals to **Xeo Quit**, a former Viet Cong base somewhat buried in the rainforest of **malucca** trees. It is now so still, the only sound to be heard is birdsong.

CAN THO

The fourth largest town in southern Vietnam and the unofficial capi-tal of the delta, **Can Tho** is known to be a university town as well as the biggest port on the Mekong River sys-tem. Situated 34km (21 miles) southwest of Vinh Long and 110km (69 miles) from the sea, Can Tho stands on the right bank of the Bas-sac at a point where the river is nearly 2km

(1.2 miles) wide. The port receives ships of up to 5000 tons and there are plans to expand handling capacity from the present 150,000 tons a year. The **river** is Can Tho's principal feature; the town's only truly memorable sight is the lively and colourful **floating market** held at the junction of seven canals.

A typical boat excursion includes the floating market where huge **wooden boats**, wholesalers loaded with mounds of cucumbers, water melons, flowers, onions, green beans, cabbages, star fruits, turnips and coconuts, sell to individuals in tiny slivers of boats that weave their way precariously in between. Typically, tours stop at a riverside **rice noodle factory** and a **rice mill** before weaving through rural canals lined with thatched shacks where children dance up and down, waving to get attention.

Alternatively, it can be pleasant simply to stroll around the town. Among the few landmarks is **Munirangsyaram Pagoda** at 36 Hoa Binh Boulevard. Built just after the war, it is a good example of the Theravada Buddhist pagodas that serve the delta's Khmer minority. **Can Tho Market** is a colourful, bustling affair paralleling the river along Hai Ba Trung Street.

Above: *Tropical forest cover in the Mekong Delta was once more extensive. Although much was destroyed during the Vietnam War when the delta provided a refuge for the Viet Cong, dense secondary rain forests have returned.*
Opposite: *Goods for sale in the shade of a colourfully decorated porticoed shopfront.*

LONG XUYEN

Some 62km (39 miles) up the Bassac from Can Tho is **Long Xuyen**, the capital of **An Giang Province**. Once the centre of the Hoa Hao religious sect, this spacious riverside town today seems somewhat wrapped up in a smug preoccupation with its reviving commercial prosperity. The one inescapable sight is an imposing, modern **Catholic church**. Perhaps of greater interest is the extremely lively and colourful **My Long Market**, located in Long Xuyen 2nd Centre and stocked by boats ferrying fresh produce across the river from the renowned fruit orchards of **Cho Moi District**.

From Long Xuyen two directions can be taken; northwest up the Bassac to Chau Doc, or southwest to Rach Gia on the coast.

CHAU DOC

Chau Doc is the last town on the Bassac before the Cambodian border 55km (34 miles) from Long Xuyen. It is a small but prosperous **commercial centre**, attractively strung out along the right bank of the **Bassac**. In town there is a charming little blue-painted **Catholic church** built in 1920. Boat excursions from here pass a village of 2,000 **floating houses** and **fish farms** – many Cambodian refugees fled here during the Khmer Rouge atrocities – to a **Cham village** across the river. There is a Muslim community centred around Chau Giang Mosque – there are no burkas here, only a few pillbox hats worn by young boys. The people speak Cham, their children study in Vietnamese at school and read the Koran in Arabic.

Particularly for Vietnamese tourists, the main attraction in this area is **Sam Mount**, about 3km (2 miles) southwest of Chau Doc. At the foot of the hill stands **Tay An Pagoda**, instantly recognized by its wildly colourful decoration. It enshrines a noted collection of some 200 wooden **religious statues**. Opposite is the **Temple of Lady Chua Xu** (Mieu Ba Chua Xu). The statue of the temple's namesake originally stood atop **Sam Mount** but was brought down in the early 19th century to be enshrined, first in a bamboo shelter and then in the present multi-roofed pagoda built in 1972. The temple's interior, sweet-smelling and heady with incense smoke, may be garish, though impressive for its crowds of

KHMER INFLUENCE

Until the middle of the 18th century, Chau Doc was part of Cambodia, and the area still supports a substantial Khmer population. Cambodia's influence is visible in the darker skin of its inhabitants and in the women's sartorial style, favouring scarves over the traditional *non la* conical hat. Chau Doc is also the seat of the Hoa Hao religion, which was founded in the nearby village of the same name in 1939.

suppliants who come to honour the holy lady and pray for good fortune before her statue. After Sam Mountain, tours stop at **Binh Duc**, a village engaged in making joss (incense) sticks from bamboo, sawdust, glue and a special ingredient that provides the scent. Daily production: 5,000 for the workshop of three; individual pay: $2.

RACH GIA

Facing the Gulf of Thailand, some 50km (30 miles) south-west of Long Xuyen, **Rach Gia** is the capital of Kien Giang Province and the delta's only significant coastal port. The town stands at the mouth of the **Cai Lon River** (the down-town area is actually an island formed by two branches of the river), and derives traditional prosperity from **fishing** and **rice cultivation**. There are a surprising number of **temples** and **pagodas**.

Phat Lon is a large 200-year-old Theravada Buddhist pagoda off Quang Trung Street on the north side of town. Also worth visiting, a short distance south at 18 Nguyen Cong Tru Street, is **Nguyen Trung Truc Temple**, dedicated to the 19th-century Vietnamese resistance fighter of the same name, executed by the French at the market place on 27 October 1868. In the centre of town, **Ong Bac De**

RACH GIA SPECIALITIES

Rach Gia is noted for its seafood and has a comparatively good selection of restaurants serving both Chinese and Vietnamese food. Other delicacies to try include cuttlefish, eel, frogs' legs, turtle and, for the less squeamish, snake.

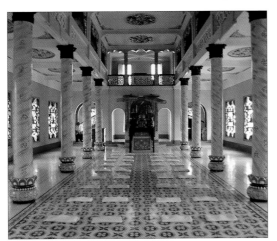

Opposite: *The delta's rich assortment of tropical fruit provides welcome refreshment.*
Left: *The symmetry, light and colour characteristic of a Cao Dai temple interior.*

Oc-Eo

Located about 10km (6 miles) inland from Rach Gia, the remains of the city of Oc-Eo, dating from the 1st to the 6th centuries AD, is the most significant archaeological site relating to the ancient Kingdom of Funan. An important trade centre, Oc-Eo has yielded finds, including Roman coins, suggestive of the scope of Funan's contacts. There are also traces of the elaborate canal systems by which Funan was able to exert material supremacy in the delta. Archaeological importance, however, is not reflected in any tourist sights and Oc-Eo has little to offer the casual visitor.

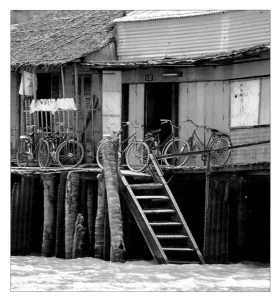

Above right: *Stilt dwellings of the Mekong Delta. Bicycles and motorbikes provide the main land transport, though there are many more waterways than roads.*

Pagoda at 14 Nguyen Du Street is a 100-year-old pagoda that was built by the local Chinese community to honour Ong Bac De, the reincarnation of the Jade Emperor of Heaven, whose imposing statue stands in the main altar.

Secular sights include a small museum at 21 Nguyen Van Troi Street, and the bustling market located at the northeast end of the island.

HA TIEN

Situated a little over 90km (56 miles) north of Rach Gia and just 6km (4 miles) from the Cambodian border, the charming little coastal town of **Ha Tien** was part of the Khmer Kingdom until the early 18th century. It is noted for a couple of 18th-century pagodas – **Tam Bao Pagoda** and **Phu Dung Pagoda** – and for its scenic setting, including nearby **beaches**. A historic town subject to perennial invasions, lastly by the Khmer Rouge in the late 1970s, Ha Tien lives on in one of the little lost corners of the world.

The Mekong Delta at a Glance

Southern Vietnam is most comfortable from **Dec–Mar**, when the weather is dry, warm and less humid.

The best way to tour the Delta is by road (with a **car** and **driver**), tourist café bus and local **boat** trips along the rivers and through the canals. **Ferries** from the wharf, at the end of Ham Nghi Boulevard in Ho Chi Minh City, take six to seven uncomfortable hours to My Tho. Roads are good to My Tho, Long Xuyen, Chau Doc and Can Tho.

Mostly by **boat**, in towns, walking or by *cyclo*.

Many cheaper hotels have only cold or tepid water.

LUXURY
Can Tho
Victoria Can Tho Hotel, Cai Khe Ward, tel: (71) 810 111, fax: (71) 829 259, e-mail: resa.cantho@victoria hotels-asia.com A delightful riverside neo-colonial atmosphere.

Chau Doc
Victoria Chau Doc Hotel, tel: (76) 865 010, fax: (76) 865 020, e-mail: resa.chau doc@victoriahotels-asia.com Luxurious neo-Victorian grandeur, exquisite food; overlooks river.

MID-RANGE
My Tho
Chuong Duong Hotel, 10 D 30/4 Street, tel: (73) 870 875, fax: (73) 874 250. My Tho's newest and best hotel, overlooking the river (inexpensive). **Hoa Binh Hotel**, 5 Hoa Binh, tel: (71) 810 218/9, fax: (71) 810 217, e-mail: hoabinhct@ hcm.vnn.vn Recently renovated and good value.

Long Xuyen
Dong Xuyen, 9A Luong Van Cu, tel: (76) 942 260, fax, (76) 942 268. Huge hotel; jacuzzi, sauna and comfortable rooms. Good value. **Hang Chau**, 10 Nguyen Van Thoai, tel: (76) 868 891, fax (76) 865 140. A good small hotel with satellite TV and air-conditioning.

BUDGET
Thuan Loi Hotel, 18 Tran Hung Dao, tel: (76) 866 134, fax: (76) 865 380. Inexpensive, river location.

Rach Gia
Phuong Hoang Hotel, 6 Nguyen Trung Truc, tel: (77) 866 525. Air conditioning, hot water, TV and fridge.

My Tho
My Tho's speciality is *hu tieu my tho*, spicy noodle soup, seafood, pork and chicken. **Cuu Long Restaurant**, tel: (73) 870 779. On the waterfront.

Can Tho
The specialty here is *ran* – snake fried in curry. **Thien Hoa Restaurant**, tel: (71) 821 942, and **Nambo Restaurant**, tel: (71) 823 908, both in Hai Ba Trung Street.

Chau Doc
The specialty here is *canh chua ca* – a sweet 'n sour fish soup. **Lam Hung Ky**, Chi Lang Street, tel: (76) 866 745, Chinese food. **My Quang Cafe**, Doc Phu Thu Street, tel: (76) 560 398.

Rach Gia
Known for its dried seafood and *nuoc mam* fish sauce. **Hoa Bien Restaurant**, Nguyen Hung Son. Seafood. **Tay Ho Restaurant**, 16 Nguyen Du, tel: (77) 863 031, good Chinese and Vietnamese food.

From **Ho Chi Minh City** (*see* excursions Chapter 6).

MEKONG DELTA	J	F	M	A	M	J	J	A	S	O	N	D
AVERAGE TEMP. °F	77	79	81	84	83	80	81	81	81	81	81	78
AVERAGE TEMP. °C	25	26	27	29	28	27	27	27	27	27	27	26
HOURS OF SUN DAILY	8	8	9	8	7	6	6	6	5	6	7	7
RAINFALL in	0	0	0	2	7	8	9	8.5	11	11	6	2
RAINFALL mm	12	22	10	50	177	206	227	217	273	277	155	41
DAYS OF RAINFALL	2	1	1	3	14	17	18	18	19	18	11	5

Travel Tips

Tourist Information

Vietnam Tourism in Hanoi and Ho Chi Minh City and **Saigon Tourist** in Ho Chi Minh City are two large, state-run organizations that deal with practicalities like visa extensions, and offer organized tours and valuable tourist information. Tourist offices in other parts of the country, many privately owned and cheaper than their state-run counterparts, are listed in the 'At a Glance' section of the relevant chapters.

Getting There

By air: Connections from Asia have exploded in the past few years. All Nippon, Asiana Airlines, China Southern Airlines, Japan Airlines, Korean Air, Lao Airlines, Lion Air, Lufthansa, Siem Reap Airways, operate flights from most Southeast Asian capitals to Vietnam, as well as the new budget carriers: Air Asia, Nok Air and Tiger Airways. THAI and Cathay Pacific also fly to Hanoi. From **Europe**: Aeroflot and Vietnam Airlines to Air France, Lufthansa and operate flights from their respective home bases to Ho Chi Minh City. From **Australia**: Vietnam Airlines and Qantas have flights linking Brisbane, Melbourne, Perth and Sydney to Ho Chi Minh City and Hanoi. From the **USA:**

United, Delta and Vietnam Airlines have direct flights from the West Coast to Vietnam.
By land: From Cambodia there are border crossings at Moc Bai-Bavet by bus and at Vinh Xuong-Kaam Samnor by boat (from Phnom Penh) or a faster more expensive boat run by Victoria Hotels (www.victoria hotels-asia.com). Also Pandaw Cruises run boats from Ho Chi Minh City to Siem Reap (www.pandaw.com). A cheaper alternative is Toum Teav Cruises (www.cfm@online.com.kh). For hearty travellers, to or from China, there are three border crossings for foreigners: Friendship Pass at Dong Dang 164 kms northeast of Hanoi, Lao Cai and Mong Cai (must arrange Chinese or Vietnamese visas in advance). From Laos, there are three border crossings at Lao Bao, Cau Treo and Na Meo. A bus runs from Danang to Savannakhet, another from Hue to Savannakhet.
By train: Twice-weekly trains run from Hanoi to Beijing. The 1,770 mile (2,950 km) trip takes 48hrs. Trains run from Hanoi to Kunming in China, 567 miles (762 km) via Lao Cai.
By sea: Cruise ships are starting to call at Vietnamese ports. Check out the latest options and availability with your local travel agency.

Airport Tax

In Hanoi the airport tax is US$14, in Ho Chi Minh City US$12, in Danang US$10. Domestic airport tax is US$2 and is paid at a separate counter prior to check-in.

Entry Requirements

All visitors must have a valid passport stamped with a visa issued by a **Vietnamese embassy**. Time needed to process a visa application varies from embassy to embassy – expect 1–2 weeks. Bangkok is the quickest and easiest place to obtain a visa. Tourist visas are normally valid for 30 days and can be extended in Vietnam for a further 15 days by major travel agents or at an Immigration Police Office (fee is usually around US$10–20). Re-entry visas are required should the traveller exit Vietnam to, for example, Cambodia, and then return. Travel agents in Vietnam can arrange re-entry visas.

Customs

Customs forms must be completed in duplicate and all valuables – such as cameras, watches and jewellery, as well as cash and travellers' cheques – must be declared. The second copy of the customs form must be kept and shown on departure. There is a **Duty Free Allowance** of 200 cigarettes or 50 cigars or 250g of tobacco, 1 litre of spirits and 1 litre of wine, along with a 'reasonable' amount of personal effects. Export of some items is restricted. This includes antiques, which may be confiscated on departure – enquire about restrictions when purchasing (but there is no guarantee).

Health Requirements

It is advisable, but not obligatory, to be vaccinated against cholera, typhoid, polio, tetanus and hepatitis. A basic medical kit should include anti-malaria tablets and strong antidiarrhoea medicine. Avoid dogs to avoid rabies. Don't drink tap water and don't eat raw fruit or vegetables. Medical standards in Vietnam, especially outside Hanoi and Ho Chi Minh City, are much lower than those in more developed countries. Greater care should be taken with hygiene, particularly in rural areas. If major medical care becomes necessary, it is best to fly to Bangkok, Singapore or Hong Kong.

Security

Pickpockets and touts are a problem, especially in Ho Chi Minh City. Otherwise, streets are generally safe. As always when travelling, watchfulness and commonsense precautions should prevail. Undetonated explosives can still be a danger in some rural areas where there was heavy fighting during the war. Keep to pathways.

What to Pack

The Vietnamese tend to dress simply and informally, both sexes favouring shirts and long trousers. While suits and ties are rarely worn, a clean, neat appearance is particularly appreciated. Shabbily dressed travellers are likely to be poorly treated. Light, natural fabrics are the most comfortable, but jumpers and coats are recommended in the north during the winter months. A sun hat in summer is useful, as is beachwear for the coastal resorts.

Accommodation

Outside of Hanoi and Ho Chi Minh City, hotels can be well below international standard, although choice and quality are improving as new joint-venture projects are being undertaken in the main cities and tourism centres. Established accommodation is for the most part adequate – clean and with the basic comforts – even if tatty and idiosyncratically furnished. Many hotels have a bewildering variety of room categories (and prices) depending on furnishing and the availability or otherwise of air-conditioning. For details of recommended establishments, consult 'At a Glance' sections at the end of each chapter.

Transport

Air: In addition to flights between Hanoi and Ho Chi Minh City, Vietnam Airlines, the national carrier, operates flights to Buon Ma Thuot, Da Lat, Da Nang, Hai Phong, Hue, Na San, Nha Trang, Pleiku, Qui Nhon, Phu Quoc Islands, Vinh, Hue, Tuy Hoa, Rach Gia, Con Son and Dien Bien Phu. Safety and service are now much improved with the acquisition of a modern fleet of Airbuses and Boeings, though domestically, late flights and cancellations still occur.

Train: A rail service operates between Hanoi and Ho Chi Minh City via Hue, Da Nang and Nha Trang. The complete journey takes two days by 'special' express and two and a half days by a 'regular' express. Train travel in Vietnam, even first class, is recommended for the adventurous only. New rail cars with air-conditioned sleeping berths and dining cars are now available on 'express' trains, but 'express' still means 30hrs from Hanoi to Ho Chi Minh City. It is, nonetheless, an enjoyable experience.

Bus: Decent reliable buses operated by the travel cafés run the length of Vietnam. Public bus service is slowly improving, but remains for those seeking a slice of life.

Hire car: Car with driver (there are as yet no self-drive rentals) is the most comfortable and convenient way to travel and is comparatively inexpensive. The state of most roads, even Highway 1, is poor, while the general standard of driving is erratic. Trucks and bicycles make up most of the traffic.

Money Matters

Currency: The dong is the official currency. It is issued in banknotes only in denominations of 200, 500, 1000, 2000, 5000, 10,000, 20,000 and 50,000.

Currency exchange: The rate of exchange fluctuates around 15,200 dong to US$1. US dollars are widely accepted – large-denomination notes get better rate of exchange, but a supply of small bills should be kept for tips, etc. Hotel reception counters also change money, usually at a fair rate. Travellers' cheques (best in US$) can be exchanged in major cities.

Credit cards: Visa and Mastercharge cards are accepted, but widespread only in Ho Chi Minh City and Hanoi.

Banks: Banking hours are Monday to Friday (08:00–11:30 and 13:00–16:00) and on Saturdays (08:00–11:30).

ATMs: Vietcombank has the largest network throughout the country. Withdrawals in dongs but withdrawals in dollars can be arranged over the counter.

Tipping: Tipping is not expected, nor is it refused. Hotels and restaurants normally add a five to 10 per cent service charge to bills. It is customary to tip guides and drivers, or in buses to collect a communal tip.

Business Hours

Government and most other offices work from Mondays to Saturdays (07:30–16:30). Lunch breaks vary from 1–2hr. Shops tend to stay open late. Nightspots close at around 23:00–23:30.

Time Difference

Vietnam is 7hr ahead of GMT.

Communications

In addition to GPOs in Hanoi and Ho Chi Minh City, major hotels offer postal, telex, fax and e-mail services. Mail can take two weeks or more to reach its destination. It is better to give outgoing mail to a departing traveller to post overseas. Leading Ho Chi Minh City hotels have IDD telephone facilities. IDD and faxes are expensive, so e-mail is the best form of communication. Web shops are plentiful.

Electricity

Most electric current is 220V/50 cycles, but 110V is also found, especially in rural areas. Beware of power surges which can affect computers and other electrical appliances. Two-pin plugs are usual, but some are flat and some round and so a multi-adapter is useful.

Etiquette

Although some Vietnamese are still cautious of meeting foreigners, most people are friendly and hospitable. In rural areas and among children especially, curiosity is often so great as to seem intentionally rude – it is not. Understanding and patience are necessary. Also, offence should not be taken at direct personal questions – one's age, income, etc. In official dealings red tape is everywhere, again, patience combined with perseverance is required. Avoid shouting, argument or displays of anger. With photography, it is common courtesy to ask permission before taking someone's picture. Shyness can lead to awkward situations and some tribal minorities may object to being photographed. The Vietnamese appreciate politeness, good manners and correct dress. With names, the correct form of address is the relevant prefix (Mr, Madame, Miss) followed by the person's given name. Vietnamese people normally have three names, the first is the family name, followed by a middle name and lastly the given name.

Festivals and Holidays

Traditional festivals remain an essential part of the culture, their celebration illustrative of the typical Vietnamese character and identity. The most important annual festivity is the

CONVERSION CHART		
FROM	**TO**	**MULTIPLY BY**
Millimetres	Inches	0.0394
Metres	Yards	1.0936
Metres	Feet	3.281
Kilometres	Miles	0.6214
Square kilometres	Square miles	0.386
Hectares	Acres	2.471
Litres	Pints	1.760
Kilograms	Pounds	2.205
Tonnes	Tons	0.984
To convert Celsius to Fahrenheit: x 9 ÷ 5 + 32		

USEFUL VIETNAMESE PHRASES

Greetings
Hello/goodbye •
Chao (formal to older
man/woman)
• *Chao ong/ba*
(less formal)
• *Chao anh/chi*
How are you?
• *(Ong/ba* or
anh/chi)
Co khoe khong?
Fine, thanks.
• *Cam on (ong/ba)*
toi van thuong.
What is your name?
• *Ten (ong/ba* or
ang/chi) la gi?
My name is…
• *Ten toi la…*
Good night
• *Chuc ngu ngon*

Useful questions
How much is it?
• *Bao nhieu?*
Where is the…?
• …*o dau?*

**Useful words and
phrases**
Yes/No • *Co/Khong*
Thank you • *Cam on*
I don't understand.
• *Toi khong hieu.*
I want/need • *Toi can*

I don't want •
Toi khong can
I like • *Toi thich*
I don't like •
Toi khong thich
I'm hungry • *Toi doi*
I'm very thirsty
• *Toi khat lam*
I'm unwell
• *Toi bi benh*

Other useful words
Bathroom • *Nha tam*
Bus • *Xe buyt*
Bus station • *Ben xe*
Cheap • *Re*
Chemist • *Nha thuoc*
Cyclo • *Xe xich-lo*
Doctor • *Bac si*
Expensive • *Dat*
Hospital • *Benh vien*
Hotel • *Khach san*
Hot water • *Nuoc
nong*
Market • *Cho*
Mountain • *Nui*
Post office • *Buu dien*
River • *Song*
Restaurant • *Nha
hang*
Telephone • *Dien
thoai*
Toilet • *Nha ve sinh*
Train station •
Ga xe lua

Food and drink
Water • *Nuoc*
Drinking water
• *Nuoc uong*
Tea • *Nuoc che*
(north), *Nuoc tra*
(south)
Coffee • *Ca phe*
Sugar • *Duong*
Beer • *Bia*
Apple • *Bom tao*
Banana • *Trai chuoi*
Beef • *Thit bo*
Butter • *Bo*
Chicken • *Thit ga*
Durian • *Trai sau
rieng*
Fish • *Ca*
Lemon • *Chanh*
Orange • *Trai cam*
Oyster • *So*
Papaya • *Trai du du*
Shrimp • *Tom*
Vegetables • *Rau*
White rice • *Com
trang*

Days of the week
Monday • *Thu hai*
Tuesday • *Thu ba*
Wednesday • *Thu tu*
Thursday • *Thu nam*
Friday • *Thu sau*
Saturday • *Thu bay*
Sunday • *Chu nhat*

Yesterday • *Hom qua*
Today • *Hom nai*
Tomorrow • *Ngay mai*
Morning • *Sang*
Evening • *Chieu*

Numbers
One • *Mot*
Two • *Hai*
Three • *Ba*
Four • *Bon*
Five • *Nam*
Six • *Sau*
Seven • *Bay*
Eight • *Tam*
Nine • *Chin*
Ten • *Muoi* or *chuc*
Eleven • *Muoi mot*
Twelve • *Muoi hai*
Twenty • *Hai muoi*
Twenty-one
• *Hai muoi mot*
Thirty • *Ba muoi*
One hundred
• *Mot tram*
Two hundred
• *Hai tram*
One thousand
• *Mot nghin*
Ten thousand
• *Muoi nghin*
One hundred thou-
sand • *Tram nghin*
One million •
Mot trieu

Lunar New Year, while other events also follow the lunar calendar. Several holidays have been added to the list of celebrations influenced by Chinese religious culture. The important events and public holidays are listed below.

1 January: Traditional New Year's Day.

Late January/Early February: Tet (Tet Nguyen Dan, meaning 'first morning of the new period') – the lunar new year and the beginning of spring celebrated from the first to the seventh day of the first lunar month. Probably the biggest celebration of the year.

3 February: The Founding of

the Communist Party of Vietnam in 1930.

March: Hai Ba Trung Day – celebrates the Trung sisters, who led a revolt against the Chinese in AD39 that held out for two years. After being defeated, the sisters committed suicide. Celebrated on the 6th day of the 2nd lunar month.

April: Thanh Minh – a festival honouring the dead, the 5th or 6th day of the 3rd lunar month.

30 April: Liberation Day – celebrates the anniversary of the day Ho Chi Minh City (Saigon) surrendered to the North Vietnamese Army.

1 May: Labour Day.

19 May: Anniversary of Ho Chi Minh's birth in the northern province of Nghe Tinh in 1890.

May/June: Anniversary of the Buddha – celebrates his birth, enlightenment and death.

August: Trung Nguyen (Wandering Souls Day) – the 15th day of the seventh lunar month marks the important festival of remembrance of the dead, with prayers and offerings to absolve sins.

2 September: National Day – commemorates Ho Chi Minh's proclamation of independence in 1945.

3 September: Ho Chi Minh's Anniversary – commemorates his death in 1969.

September/October:
Trung Thu (Mid-Autumn Festival) is on the 15th day of the eighth lunar month. Traditional features of the festival are rice moon cakes and decorated, brightly coloured lanterns.

November: Confucius's birthday – celebrated on 28th day of the ninth month.

25 December: Christmas Day – although it is not an official holiday.

Hanoi
Hanoi Tourism: 18B Ly Thuong Kiet Street, tel: (4) 826-6714.
Vietnam Tourism: 30A Ly Thuong Kiet Street, tel: (4) 826-4154.
Ho Chi Minh City
Saigon Tourist: 23 Le Loi Street, District 1, tel: (8) 822-5887.
Vietnam Tourism: 234 Nam Ky Khoi Nghia, District 3, tel: (8) 829-2442.

Language
Tonal and monosyllabic, Vietnamese is a difficult language for Westerners to master. Five tones are used in the south, six in the north, and every syllable is inflected by a tone, which determines the meaning. Thus words sounding the same to an untrained ear may have five (or six) different meanings. French is spoken by many of the older Vietnamese, while English is gaining in popularity. German and Russian are understood to a lesser extent, especially in the south. The language barrier can be a problem, and although foreigners can muddle through, a few Vietnamese words can be useful and courteous. Bilingual dictionaries (English–Vietnamese and Vietnamese–English) are easily obtainable in Ho Chi Minh City and Hanoi and, for the more ambitious, courses in the language are run in Ho Chi Minh City.

GOOD READING

Borton, Lady (1995) *After Sorrow: An American among the Vietnamese*. A moving account of an American woman's experiences when she shares the life of two villages, North and South, in the 90s. New York.
Duong Thu Huong (2000) *Memories of a Pure Spring*. A fictional account of how a singer and her composer husband struggle to survive in modern Vietnam. Picador, New York.
Fitzgerald, Francis (1972) *Fire in the Lake*. Multiple prize-winning account of US involvement in Vietnam.New York.
Greene, Graham *The Quiet American* (1955). A classic and prophetic modern novel of Vietnam at the end of the French conflict and the beginning of American involvement. London.
Herr, Michael (1977) *Dispatches*. A superbly readable 'new journalism' account of the war. New York.
Huu Ngoc (1997) *Sketches for a Portrait of Vietnamese Culture*. An in-depth analysis of how Vietnam's history and literature have shaped the nation. The Gioi Publishers, Hanoi.
Lewis, Norman (1951) *Dragon Apparent*. One of the best travel books on Vietnam – a classic. London.
Sheehan, Neil (1988) *A Bright Shining Lie: John Paul Vann and Americans in Vietnam*. A highly acclaimed biographical account of the USA and the war; Pulitzer and National Book Award winner. New York.

INDEX

Note: Numbers in **bold** indicate photographs

accommodation 5, 39, 44, 46–47, 58–59, 62, 63, 70, 81, 82–83, 85, 86, 93, 95, 97, **98**, 100, 108–109, 111, 121, 123
agriculture 5, **7**, 11, 16, 19, 22, **24**, 26, 55, 62, **92**, 94, **112**, 113, 114, 115, 117, 119
An Giang Province 117
architecture 30, 31, 35, 36, 41, 42, **52**, 65, 70, 75, **79**, 80, 88, 99, 100, **102**
art 30–32, 44, 70, 75–76, 101, 103

Ba Be Lake 11, 49, 54–55
Ba Dinh 36, 40–42
Bac Can 54, 55
Bai Chay 50, 51
Ban Doc Waterfall 55
Bao Dai 20, 63, 68, 69, 88–89, 94
beaches 7, **8**, 62, 63, 76, 85, 120
  Cau Dai 78
  China **76**
  Doc Let 89
  Mui Ne 106–**107**
  Nha Trang **84**, 86, 87, 88
Binh Duc 119–120
Buon Ma Thuot 85, 90

camping 53
Can Tho 111, 114, 117
Cat Ba Island 49, 53
cathedrals
  Da Lat Cathedral 93
  Da Nang Cathedral 77
  Nha Tho Lon (see St Joseph's Cathedral)
  Nha Trang Cathedral 88
  Notre Dame Cathedral **28**, 71, 100
  Phu Cam Cathedral 71
  St Joseph's Cathedral 43
Central Highlands 7, 82–83, 85, 91, **92**
Champa 13, 14–16, 17, 57
Chams 7, 16, 17, 25, 61–64, 75–77, 81, 85, 87, **88**, 97, 107, 114, 118

Chau Doc 111, 114, 118–119
Chau Xuong 79
China 8, 12, 13, 14, 15, 16, 17, 18, 49, 62, 97, 114
Cho Moi District 118
Cholon 98, 101, **103**–104
citadels 5, 35, 36, 41, 45, 55, 61, 64, **65**, 66, **69**
climate 6, 8–9, 36, 46, 51, 58, 62, 73, 82, 86, 91, 95, 98, 107, 113, 108, 121
Cochinchina 13, 19, 97
Cold War 20
communications 124
Communism 19, 20, 22
conservation 10–11, 61
contacts 47
crafts 37–38, 45, 103
Cu Chi Tunnels 97, 105
Cuc Phuong 11, 55
culture 6, 8, 14, 25, 30, **31**–32, 40, 42, 67, 99
currency 123, 124
customs 122
cyclos (bicycle trishaws) 78, 98

Da Lat 7, 85, **91**, **92**–**93**, 94
Da Nang 7, 16, 19, **26**, 31, 62, 74–77
Dac Lac Province 90
Dai Nghien 37
Dau Dang Waterfall 55
democracy 23
Dien Bien Phu 49, 52, 54, 66
Dien Thai Hoa (see Palace of Supreme Harmony)
DMZ 57, 79
doi moi (new thinking) 13, 23, 98
Du Khiem Pavilion 73
dynasties
  Dinh 17
  Han 13
  Ho 13, 17, 41,
  Hung 11, 68
  Le 13, 16, 17, 40, 55
  Ming 17
  Ngo 16, 17, 66
  Nguyen 17, 18, 35, 61, 62, 64, 65, 66, 67, 68, 70, 73, 90, 113
  Tang 15, 16
  Tran 13, 16, 17, 37, 101
economy **22**–24, 75, 98

fauna 9–11, 73, 90
festivals 45, 124–125
Flag Tower 40, 65
food 6, **9**–11, **32**, **33**, 73, 86, 107, 114, 116, **118**, 119,
Forbidden Purple City 63, 65, 67
forests 9, 10
French colonialism 7, 10, 13, 18, **19**–22, 24, 29, 36, 42, 61, 62, 63, 64, 68, 70, 74, 75, 77, 91, 92, 97, 99, 100, 105, 114
Funan 14–16, 112, 120

General Post Office 100
Gia Long 18, 19, 65, 67, 69
government 22–24

Ha Long Bay 5, 49, **50**–**51**, 56
Ha Tien 111, 120
Haiphong 51–52
Hai Van Pass **60**, 62, 74
Hanoi 7, 9, 11, 13, 16, 17, 21, 32, 35, 37, **39**, 46–47, 74, 98
health 123
Highway 1 7, **56**, 57, 61, 91
history 11–22, 41, 78, 101, 103, 113
Ho Chi Minh 13, **18**, 19, 20, 31, 42, 43, 57, 66, 72, 100
Ho Chi Minh City 7, 8, **28**, 35, 61, 63, 70, 74, 91, **96**, 97–107, 108–109, 114
Ho Chi Minh's Mausoleum 35, 41
Hoa Binh **48**
Hoa Lu 35, 55, 56
Hoan Kiem Lake 36, **37**, 39
Hoang Trach Gate 73
Hoi An 5, 7, 62, 74, **78**–**79**, **80**
Hon Chong Promontory 85, 88
Hue 5, 7, 11, 13, 16, 18, 35, 49, 61, 62–69
Imperial City 63, 65, 66, 67
imperial tombs 5, 61, 68, 71–**72**, **73**–74
independence 15, 20
India 15, 16, 62
Indo-China 19, 35, 42, 90

Japan 20, 24, 62, 63, 80, 98
Japanese Covered Bridge **80**

Khmer 15, 16, 18, 25, 61, 62, 114, 118
Kon Tum 85, 90
Kublai Khan 17, 37
Ky Dai (see Flag Tower) 65

Lac Viets 11, 13
Lake of Sighs 94
land 6–11
Lang Son 50, 55, 56
language 25, 26–27, 126
Laos 19, 52, 75
literature 32, 125
Long Xuyen 114, 117–118
Luu Khiem Lake 73
Ly Thai Tho 39, 41

markets 37, **45**, 53, 54, **92**, **96**, 98, 103, 104, 105, 114, 117, 118
Da Lat 93
Dong Ba **24**, 69
Hoi An 79
Mekong Delta 5, 6, **7**, 8, **10**, 11, 15, 16, 18, 25, 61, 97, 111–**113**, 114–**117**, 118–**120**, 121
Minh Mang 65, 67, 69
minorities 49, 53, **54**, **55**, 90
money (see currency)
montagnards (the highland people) 25, 49, 85, 90, 92
mountains
  Bach Ma 73
  Fansipan 53
  Lang Bian 94
  Marble 77
  Nui Ba Den 107
  Tam Dao 44
  Truong Son 7, 49, 61, 85
Mui Ne 7, 97, **106**
Municipal Theatre **43**, 99
Municipal Water Puppet Theatre 39
museums 57, 87, 120
  Bao Tang Cham (see Museum of Cham Sculpture)
  Chi Lai Communal House 52
  Da Nang's Museum of Cham Sculpture **14**, 31
  Fine Arts Museum 43, 100

museums (cont.)
  Hanoi's new Museum of
    Ethnography 35
  History Museum 40, 97,
    100, 101
  Ho Chi Minh Museum 40,
    42, 71, 100
  Imperial Museum 71
  Museum of Cham
    Sculpture 61, 75–76
  Museum of Ethnography
    40, 54
  Museum of Ho Chi Minh
    City 100
  The Ethnographic Museum
    90
  War Remnants Museum
    100, 101
  Womens' Museum 40
My Son 61, 62, 81
My Tho **30**, 111, **114**,
  115–116

Nam Viet 12, 13, 19
national parks 10–11, 73,
  90
Ngo Dinh Diem 13, 20, 70,
  88, 104
Ngoan Muc Pass 85, 91
Nha Trang 5, 6, 7, 85,
  86–88, **89**, 90, 94
nine dynastic urns 67, **69**
North Gate 40

Oc-Eo 15, 120
Old East Gate 39
Old Quarter **34**, 35, 36,
  37–38
Old Town (see Old Quarter)
Opera House (see Municipal
  Theatre)

Pac Ngoi village 54–55
pagodas
  Ambassador (see Chua
    Quan Su)
  Ba Da 43
  Bao Quoc 71
  Chua Huong Tich 5, 35,
    44–45
  Chua Ong 69
  Chua Quan Su 44
  Chuc Thanh 80
  Dai Hanh 55
  Dien Huu 41
  Dieu De National 69
  Dinh Tien Hoang 55
  Du Hang Pagoda 52
  Emperor of Jade 101

pagodas (cont.)
  Fragrant Perfume (see
    Chua Huong Tich)
  Giac Lam 97, 102
  Giac Vien 102
  Giai Oan Chua 44
  Kiep Bac 53
  Linh Son 93
  Linh Ung 77
  Long Song 88
  Munirangsyaram 117
  Nghia An Hoi Quan **104**
  One Pillar 40, **41**
  Ong Bac De 120
  Phap Lam **26**, 77
  Pho Da 76
  Phu Dung 120
  Phuoc Lam 80
  Purgatory (see Giai Oan
    Chua)
  Quan Am 104
  Quan Am Tu 93
  Quan Thanh 41
  Tam Bao 76, 120
  Tam Son Hoi Quan Pagoda
    104
  Tam Thai 77
  Tay An 118
  Tay Phuong 45
  Thay 45
  Thiem Chua 44
  Thien Hau 104
  Thien Mu **4**, 63, 69–**70**
  Thien Vuong 93
  Tortoise 37
  Tran Quoc **40**, 41
  Tu Dam 71
  Vinh Nghiem 102
  Vinh Trang **30**, 116
  West (see Tay Phuong)
  Xa Loi 103
  Palace of Supreme Harmony
    66–67
Paracel Islands 8
people 25–33
Phan Rang **15**, 16, 76, 91,
  97
Phung Island 115
Po Klong Garai Towers 93
Po Nagar Cham Towers 87
population 6, 25, 91, 114
Presidential Palace 42

Quan An 41, 70
Quang Tri Province 57

Rach Gia 114, 119
Red River Delta 6, 7, 11, 12,
  13, 21, 36, 49, **50**, 112

religion 27–30, **88**, 114, 115
  Animism 27
  Buddhism 14, 20, 27, 70,
    76, 77, 88, 94, 102, 103,
    114
  Cao Daism 29–30
  Catholicism 27, 56, 114,
    116, 118
  Christianity 28, 29, 93,
    104
  Confucianism **12**, 14, 16,
    18, 27, 28–29, 42
  Hao 27, 29–30, 118
  Hinduism 15, 29, 76, **81**,
    87, 102
  Islam 8, 27, 29, 102, 114
  Taoism 14, 27, 28–29, 102
resorts 5, 52, 77, 85, 86, 89,
  107
restaurants 5, 46, 59, 63,
  70, 77, 83, 86, 93, 95,
  98, 109, 121
Reunification Palace 97, 100
rivers 111
  Bach Dang 16, 52
  Bassac 111, 118
  Ben Hai 57
  Cai 87
  Cai Lon 119
  Cam 51
  Cuu Long Giang 112
  Han 74
  Mekong 62, 111–120
  Nang 54
  Ngo Dong 56
  Perfume 5, 6, 61, 62–**63**,
    67, 69, 70, 71
  Red 61
  Saigon **98**, **101**
  Song Huong (see Perfume)
  Thu Bon 62, 77, **78**
  Yen 44

Sa Pa 49, 50, **52**, 53, 55
Saigon (see Ho Cho Minh
  City)
Sam Mount 111, 118
shopping 37–38, 47, 79, 83,
  98, 103, **116**
South China Sea 6, 8, 74,
  98, 112
sport 6, 85, 89, **94**
Spratly Islands 8

Tam Coc 55, 56
Tan Long 111, 115
Tay Ninh 56, 105–106
Tay Son rebellion 13, 17,
  18, 64, 66, 78

temples 61, 63, 67, 75,
  101–**102**, 103, 105, 106,
  119
  Cao Dai Temple 77, 97,
    114, **119**
  Den Bach Ma 38–39
  Hoa Khiem Temple 73
  Huyen Khong Cave 77
  Ngoc Son **37**
  Nguyen Trung Truc 119
  Quan Am 79
  Quan Cong 79
  Sung An 73
  Temple of Lady Chua Xu
    118
  Van Mieu 5, **12**, 13, **16**,
    35, 41–42
  White Horse (see Den
    Bach Ma Temple)
Tet Offensive 64, 65, 67, 69,
  107
Thailand 8, 62, 114
Than Thai 68, 69
Thien Nan **26**
Thieu Tri 69, 70
Thong Nhat Conference Hall
  (see Reunification Palace)
Tien Gian Province 115
To Mieu 67, 68
tourist cafés 56, 63
tours 47, 49, 50, 59, 83, 89,
  105–107, 109, 95, 114,
  115, 121
transport 7, 46, 58, 82, 95,
  108, 121, 122, 123
tribes 85, 88, 90, 94
Trinh 17, 67
Tu Cam Thanh (see
  Forbidden Purple City)
Tu Duc 69, 73

U-Minh forest 10, 112, 116
USA 13, 20, 21, 24, 62, 63,
  64, 75, 79, 87, 97, 98,
  105

Viet Cong **117**
Viet Minh 20, 52, 54, 105
Vinh Long 114, 116

war 6, 11–22, 51, 62, 63,
  64, 75, 79, 81, 85, 87,
  91, 97, 101, 107, 113,
  114, 115, 116
water puppets 5, 6, **32**, 35,
  39, 42, 45
West Lake **40**–42

Xuan Huong Lake 92, 94

GLOBETROTTER™

Travel Guide

ALINSKAS

VIETNAM

JOHN HOSKIN AND
CAROL HOWLAND

NEW
HOLLAND

NEW
HOLLAND

★★★ Highly recommended
★★ Recommended
★ See if you can

Fourth edition published in 2006
by New Holland Publishers (UK) Ltd
London • Cape Town • Sydney • Auckland
First published in 1995
10 9 8 7 6 5 4 3 2 1

website: www.newhollandpublishers.com

Garfield House,
86 Edgware Road
London W2 2EA,
United Kingdom

80 McKenzie Street
Cape Town 8001,
South Africa

14 Aquatic Drive,
Frenchs Forest,
NSW 2086, Australia

218 Lake Road, Northcote,
Auckland, New Zealand

Distributed in the USA by
The Globe Pequot Press, Connecticut

ISBN 1 84537 551 3

Although every effort has been made to ensure that
this guide is up to date and current at time of going
to print, the Publisher accepts no responsibility or
liability for any loss, injury or inconvenience incurred
by readers or travellers using this guide.

Publishing Manager: Thea Grobbelaar
DTP Cartographic Manager: Genené Hart
Editors: Nicky Steenkamp, Melany McCallum,
Jacqueline de Vos, Brigitte Lee
Cartographers: Tanja Spinola, Nicole Bannister
Design and DTP: Nicole Bannister, Lellyn Creamer,
Philip Mann, ACE Ltd.
Picture Researchers: Shavonne Johannes,
Colleen Abrahams

Reproduction by Hirt & Carter (Pty) Ltd, Cape Town
Printed and bound by Times Offset (M) Sdn. Bhd., Malaysia.

Photographic Credits:
Anders Blomqvist: title page, pages 63, 94;
Jill Gocher: pages 12, 14, 18, 20, 31 (top), 54, 56, 84,
88, 89, 101;
Tim Hall: pages 7, 15, 21, 22, 23, 27, 31 (bottom),
32 (bottom), 36, 65, 66, 72, 73, 78, 86, 98, 101, 103, 114;
Lois Hechenblaikner: pages 8, 10, 24 (bottom), 30, 33, 51,
52, 92 (top and bottom), 115, 117;
Carol Howland: pages 26, 66, 91, 93, 106, 107;
Hutchison Image Library/Christine Pemberton: page 4;
Photonica/Photo Access: cover;
Shari Kessler: pages 16, 17, 19, 24 (top), 25, 32 (top), 37,
39, 42, 48, 51 (bottom), 55, 57, 79, 80 (top and bottom),
81, 112;
Valerie Martin: page 77;
Alain Proust: pages 9, 27, 28, 41, 45, 60, 70, 75, 76, 96,
104, 105, 110, 113, 116, 118, 119, 120;
Neil Setchfield: pages 34, 50.

Keep us Current
Information in travel guides is apt to change, which is
why we regularly update our guides. We'd be grateful
to receive feedback if you've noted something we
should include in our updates. If you have new
information, please share it with us by writing to the
Publishing Manager, Globetrotter, at the office nearest
to you (addresses on this page). The most significant
contribution to each new edition will receive a free
copy of the updated guide.

Cover: *A decorative temple in the Forbidden Purple
City in Hue, Vietnam.*
Title page: *A set of water puppets represents a
microcosm of Vietnamese society.*